Entrepreneurship in the UK

David G. Blanchflower

Bruce V. Rauner Professor of Economics
Dartmouth College
University of Stirling
Bank of England
UK
david.blanchflower@bankofengland.co.uk

Chris Shadforth

External Monetary Policy Committee Unit
Bank of England
UK
chris.shadforth@bankofengland.co.uk

the essence of knowledge

Boston – Delft

Foundations and Trends® in Entrepreneurship

Published, sold and distributed by:
now Publishers Inc.
PO Box 1024
Hanover, MA 02339
USA
Tel. +1-781-985-4510
www.nowpublishers.com
sales@nowpublishers.com

Outside North America:
now Publishers Inc.
PO Box 179
2600 AD Delft
The Netherlands
Tel. +31-6-51115274

The preferred citation for this publication is D. G. Blanchflower and C. Shadforth, Entrepreneurship in the UK, Foundations and Trends® in Entrepreneurship, vol 3, no 4, pp 257–364, 2007

ISBN: 978-1-60198-038-0
© 2007 D. G. Blanchflower and C. Shadforth

Foundations and Trends® in Entrepreneurship
Volume 3 Issue 4, 2007
Editorial Board

Editorial Scope

Foundations and Trends® in Entrepreneurship will publish survey and tutorial articles in the following topics:

- Nascent and start-up entrepreneurs
- Opportunity recognition
- New venture creation process
- Business formation
- Firm ownership
- Market value and firm growth
- Franchising
- Managerial characteristics and behavior of entrepreneurs
- Strategic alliances and networks
- Government programs and public policy
- Gender and ethnicity
- New business financing:

- Business angels
- Bank financing, debt, and trade credit
- Venture capital and private equity capital
- Public equity and IPO's
- Family-owned firms
- Management structure, governance and performance
- Corporate entrepreneurship
- High technology
- Technology-based new firms
- High-tech clusters
- Small business and economic growth

Information for Librarians

Foundations and Trends® in Entrepreneurship, 2007, Volume 3, 4 issues. ISSN paper version 1551-3114. ISSN online version 1551-3122. Also available as a combined paper and online subscription.

Foundations and Trends® in
Entrepreneurship
Vol. 3, No. 4 (2007) 257–364
© 2007 D. G. Blanchflower and C. Shadforth
DOI: 10.1561/0300000017

Entrepreneurship in the UK

David G. Blanchflower[1] and Chris Shadforth[2]

[1] Bruce V. Rauner Professor of Economics, Dartmouth College, University
of Stirling, NBER, IZA and Member of the Monetary Policy Committee,
Bank of England, blanchflower@dartmouth.edu;
david.blanchflower@bankofengland.co.uk; www.dartmouth.edu/~blnchflr
[2] External Monetary Policy Committee Unit, Bank of England,
chris.shadforth@bankofengland.co.uk

Abstract

This paper examines the causes and consequences of changes in the
incidence of entrepreneurship in the UK. Self-employment as a proportion of total employment is high by international standards in the UK,
but the share has fluctuated over time. We examine the time series
movements in self-employment, which are principally driven by financial liberalization and changes in taxation rules, especially as they relate
to the construction sector which is the dominant sector. We document
that the median earnings of the self-employed is less than for employees. We show that in comparison with employees the self-employed are
more likely to be males; immigrants; work in construction or financial
activities; hold an apprenticeship; work in London; work long hours;
have high levels of job satisfaction and happiness. Consistent with the
existence of capital constraints on potential and actual entrepreneurs,
the estimates imply that the probability of self-employment depends

positively upon whether the individual ever received an inheritance or gift. Evidence is also found that rising house prices have increased the self-employment rate. There appears to be no evidence that changes in self-employment are correlated with changes in real GDP, nor national happiness.

Contents

1

Introduction

This paper examines the causes and consequences of changes in the incidence of entrepreneurship in the UK. But an initial question must be: how many entrepreneurs are there? The answer is not straightforward. There are several ways of counting them. The simplest is to count the number of self-employed workers, but even that is difficult. We could count those that self-report their employment status, such as in the Labour Force Survey (LFS).[1] Or we could count the number of individuals who declare self-employment income for taxation purposes. It would be useful to do both and see if the numbers equate. They do not. In fact, the number of people who declare taxable income from self-employment in the UK is roughly 50% greater than the number that say they are self-employed. Her Majesty's Revenue and Customs (HMRC) records just over 4.5 million individuals declaring some income from

---

[1] The definition of self-employment in the Labour Force Survey is left entirely to the respondent, and with no guidance or prompt. This could result in a lack of coherence with other measures of the self-employed, such as the Inland Revenue's Survey of Personal Incomes (SPI) or with measures of jobs based largely on employer surveys, such as workforce jobs. There is currently a consistency check to the LFS, carried out by the ONS, which recodes some respondents' employment status to employee if the occupation they claim to do is inconsistent with self-employment (for example, self-employed policeman).

self-employment in 2003/2004, but the LFS records just over 3 million self-employed workers. This is not that surprising.

It is clear that many individuals have more than one job, so the number of individuals reporting self-employed earnings for taxation purposes should be expected to be higher than the number that say they are self-employed. It is also likely that in some instances individuals will struggle to identify whether they are principally an employee or self-employed. They could base their decision on hours worked or income earned. Or it could reflect the timing of survey responses. A classic example is that of a free-lancing actor. Fifty-one weeks of the year they work for a wage waiting tables in a restaurant. But by the survey reference week they have quit their job as a waiter and they star in a film for which they are paid one hundred times the wages they earned as a waiter over the previous 51 weeks. Are they self-employed or employed?

In this paper, we focus primarily on the characteristics of the self-employed and how self-employment has changed over time, principally in the UK, using the LFS. Unfortunately these data do not record self-employed earnings. Consequently, we also make use of the HMRC data as well as information from various Family Resources Surveys to compare earnings of the self-employed with the wages and salaries earned by employees.

The most entrepreneurial individuals in the UK, such as Lakshmi Mittal, Sir Richard Branson and Sir Alan Sugar, are generally not included in our surveys. A very small number of the most entrepreneurial individuals are very important both in terms of wealth and job creation. What distinguishes them from everyone else? As far as we can, with the limited data available, we examine their characteristics too.

In what follows we first consider time series trends in self-employment in the UK and elsewhere. Second, we compare the earnings of the self-employed with those of wage and salary workers. Third, we examine the characteristics of the self-employed. Fourth, we perform a series of econometric analyses of the determinants of self-employment and draw comparisons with the US and the EU. Fifth, we consider the importance of liquidity constraints and the role of inheritances and gifts and rising house prices in overcoming these credit constraints. Sixth, we examine macro-economic consequences and correlates of self-employment and draw a series of conclusions. The aim of this paper is thus to identify the characteristics of the self-employed and try to explain how and why their numbers have changed over time.

2

Time Series Trends

Self-employment as a proportion of total UK employment is high in comparison with other OECD countries (Blanchflower, 2000, 2004).[1] Table A.1 reports data on the change in the proportion of all workers who were self-employed in the decades since the 1960s for the OECD countries (Australia, Austria, Belgium, Canada, Czech Republic, Denmark, Finland, France, Germany, Greece, Hungary, Iceland, Ireland, Italy, Japan, Korea, Luxembourg, Mexico, the Netherlands, New Zealand, Norway, Poland, Portugal, Slovakia, Spain, Sweden, Switzerland, Turkey, UK, USA). Data are taken from the *OECD Labour Force Statistics*. In the 1960s, the highest proportions were found in Italy (36.4%), Korea (35.0%), Poland (34.5%), Ireland (30.1%), and Austria (28.3%). The proportion of self-employed workers has subsequently fallen sharply in all these countries, and most others. The only countries to have recorded increases in their self-employment rates between the 1960s and 2000s (for which data are available) have been the UK and New Zealand. The Norwegian rate did increase by 0.7pp, but has

---

[1] Alternatively, the total workforce can be used as the denominator, as in Weir (2003) or Taylor (2004). Movements in the two series appear very similar over time.

actually been falling since the 1970s. The increase in the UK was +5.2pp while the increase in New Zealand was 4.7pp.

A similar result holds in Table A.2 for *non-agricultural* self-employment in these two countries. However, there are now several additional countries for which the trend has been upwards over the past 4 decades (or 3 where data for the 1960s is not available): Australia, Canada, Finland, Germany, Iceland, Ireland, Mexico, the Netherlands, Poland, Portugal, and Sweden. Within these other countries it would appear that declines in agricultural self-employment have shrouded an upward trend in self-employment across other sectors. Moreover, the self-employment rate falls by less (or increases in the case of those countries previously mentioned) across 24 of the 25 countries for which data are available when only those employed in non-agricultural activities are considered; the exception being Mexico. The difference is most apparent in Poland, where the average non-agricultural self-employment rate was +9.0pp higher in the 2000s than the average of the 1960s, compared with a −12.6pp fall when all workers are considered. The change in the UK self-employment rate excluding agricultural workers is little different from that including those workers. But the change in the New Zealand rate is nearly twice as large (+7.7pp vs. +4.7pp) when only those employed in non-agricultural activities are considered.

Table A.3 sets out a time series of self-employment rates for the UK, based on data published in various issues of the Employment Gazette between 1962 and 1991 (collected by the Department of Employment and Productivity (1962–1970); and the Department of Employment (1971–1991)), and subsequently data from the UK LFS. In 2006, out of 28,959,000 workers, 3,753,000 or 13.0% of the labor force were classified as self-employed. This figure has increased markedly in recent years, up from 11.9% in 2001. Between 2001 and 2006, the number of employees increased by 3.5%, while the number of self-employed workers increased by 13.7%. The self-employment rate has been higher than this, however. The rate peaked at just over 14% in 1991, and remained around 13.5% during much of the early 1990s, before gradually declining from 1997. But prior to the 1990s, the rate had been much lower. Using OECD data, the average self-employment rate in the UK during the

1960s was 7.1%; the 1970s, 8.0%; the 1980s, 10.8%; the 1990s, 13.3%; and the 2000s, 12.3%. These averages clearly indicate that the period of most rapid growth in UK self-employment was during the 1980s. As a validation of the changes in self-employment it is appropriate to look at VAT registrations published by the Department of Trade and Industry (DTI).[2] VAT registrations and deregistrations, according to the DTI, are "the best official guide to the pattern of business start-ups and closures".[3] The VAT figures do not, however, give the complete picture of start-up and closure activity in the economy. Some VAT exempt sectors and businesses operating below the threshold for VAT registration are not covered. At the start of 2005, the VAT threshold was an annual turnover of £58,000, and only 1.8 million of the estimated 4.3 million enterprises in the UK were VAT-registered. However, some businesses do voluntarily register for VAT even though their turnover is below the threshold. Data for 2005 shows that around a fifth of all registrations had turnover below the VAT threshold.

In 2005 there were 177,900 registrations and 152,900 de-registrations, resulting in an increase of 25,000 (1.4%) in the stock of VAT registered enterprises. As can be seen in Table 2.1, there have been increases in the stock of VAT registrations in every year from 1995.

Chart A.1 shows that these movements in VAT registrations loosely track the changes in self-employment shown in Table A.3 – the correlation is +0.60.[4] On both measures there were marked declines in the period 1991–1994. However, the two series move in opposite directions between 1995 and 2002. The decline in the self-employment rate is primarily related to changes in the rules of the Construction Industry Scheme (CIS), which is the Inland Revenue's taxation system for the construction industry. Freedman (2001) noted that between 1995 and 1997, 200,000 construction workers reclassified themselves as employees as a result of changes to the CIS. We discuss the impact of changes in the CIS in more detail below.

---

[2] The VAT data were also examined by Black et al. (1996).

[3] "Business start-ups and closures: VAT registrations and de-registrations in 2005," DTI, http://www.dtistats.net/smes/vat/VATStatsPressReleaseOct2006.pdf.

[4] Note that increases in the VAT registration threshold in 1991 and 1993 mean the estimates are only broadly comparable over the period 1980–2005.

Table 2.1

	Registrations	Deregistrations	Net change
1980	160,550	145,270	15,280
1981	154,135	122,590	31,545
1982	168,280	148,315	19,965
1983	182,550	148,080	34,470
1984	184,575	155,085	29,490
1985	184,865	166,760	18,105
1986	193,755	169,070	24,685
1987	211,795	172,580	39,215
1988	245,800	179,650	66,150
1989	258,840	181,005	77,835
1990	239,105	191,840	47,265
1991	204,565	209,845	−5,280
1992	187,000	226,000	−39,000
1993	191,000	213,000	−22,000
1994	166,870	173,610	−6,740
1995	161,750	161,305	445
1996	166,050	150,935	15,115
1997	182,680	145,950	36,730
1998	182,205	145,750	36,455
1999	176,915	150,310	26,605
2000	178,905	155,755	23,150
2001	170,015	155,890	14,125
2002	176,920	162,405	14,515
2003	191,220	165,530	25,690
2004	183,780	163,400	20,380
2005	177,925	152,945	24,980

Source: DTI, http://www.dtistats.net/smes/vat/.

It is also apparent that there have been significant changes in the size distribution of firms registered for VAT. Table 2.2 shows that the *number* of firms increased by nearly 620,000 between 2000 and 2005, of which just over 570,000 (92.1%) were firms with no employees.

Table A.4 reports survival rates of VAT registered enterprises for up to 10 years for the UK from 1995 to 2005. The probability of a firm surviving 10 years is approximately one-third. Over time the probability of survival has increased.

The late 1980s account for most of the increase in the number of entrepreneurs in the UK economy – whether we define entrepreneurship using self-employment numbers or VAT registrations. The number of self-employed workers rose by more than 230,000 in each of the years 1986–1987, 1988–1989, and 1989–1990, while the 1987–1988 increase was a still healthy, 150,000. So between 1986 and 1990 the number of

Table 2.2

	2005	2000
All enterprises	4,342,045	3,722,610
With no employees	3,162,600	2,591,775
All employers	1,179,445	1,130,835
1–4	778,700	738,685
5–9	207,225	206,090
10–19	106,020	108,075
20–49	54,955	46,155
50–99	17,160	15,700
100–199	7,835	7,820
200–249	1,575	1,565
250–499	3,030	3,260
500 or more	2,940	3,485

Source: DTI, http://www.dtistats.net/smes/sme/.

self-employed grew by over 850,000, from 2.91 million to 3.76 million, while the rate grew from 11.8% to 14.0%. It is apparent that 1984 was also an important year for growth, with the largest (+266k) annual increase on record.

Sharp falls in both self-employment and VAT registrations followed in the early 1990s, contemporaneous with the UK recession. The number of self-employed workers fell by −91k in 1991–1992, −208k in 1992–1993, and −58k in 1993–1994. It is notable, however, that the self-employment rate did not start to fall until 1992, while the unemployment rate started to rise in late 1990. This indicates that employees felt the effects of the downturn in demand earlier than the self-employed. The self-employment rate then stabilized for a period, before falling again.

The number of self-employed workers declined in all but two years between 1990 and 2000. This decline was dramatically reversed in 2003, when the number of self-employed workers rose by +229k. A further 100k individuals became self-employed in 2006, causing the self-employment rate to rise to 13.0%. VAT registrations also fell between 1997 and 2001, and then increased subsequently.

The big increases in self employment in the late-1980s occurred as unemployment was declining sharply, while the falls of the early 1990s occurred as the labor market loosened. In contrast, the 2001–2004 increase of more than 300,000, alongside a jump of nearly 1% point in the rate (11.9% in 2001 to 12.8% in 2004), seems rather large given that the unemployment rate declined by only 0.4pp, from 5.2% to 4.8%, over this period. So how is self-employment related to the economic cycle?

It is well established that the employment rate tends to move pro-cyclically, while the unemployment rate typically moves in the opposite direction. This inverse relationship is very simple to explain. Every individual in the population (Pop) can be categorized into three groups: employed (E), unemployed (U) or inactive (I). We can therefore write:

$$E + U + I = Pop. \tag{2.1}$$

By dividing through by population and substituting the standard definitions for the employment rate ($e = E/Pop$), unemployment rate ($u = U/(U+E)$), and the activity rate ($a = (U+E)/Pop$) into Equation (2.1), we can state:

$$e = a(1 - u). \tag{2.2}$$

This says that the employment rate should be negatively correlated with the unemployment rate given stable activity; which it is.

Self-employment is a significant component of total employment, so one might imagine that movements in the self-employment rate should also be closely (inversely) correlated with movements in the unemployment rate. But such a relationship is not clear in the UK. Chart A.2 shows that while there was a strong negative correlation between 1984 and 1994 (−0.75), the correlation over the 35 years since 1971 has been positive (+0.41). Furthermore, Chart A.3 shows that the self-employment rate and total employment rate are actually *negatively* correlated over the same period. In other words, the self-employment rate is not well correlated with the economic cycle and the inverse relationship between employment and unemployment between 1971 and 1984, and since 1994, is driven entirely by forms of employment other than self-employment. Why might this occur?

There are two distinct types of self-employed workers: those that choose ("pulled") to become self-employed because of economic prosperity; and those that are pushed into self-employment because of economic adversity. Chart A.4 captures the rate of transition of workers "pulled" into self-employment over the economic cycle using microdata from the LFS. The transition rate clearly rises in periods of economic expansion. For example, 8.2% of self-employed workers in 2006 had been employees in 2005. This translates into a flow of 308,000 workers. This may seem high, but one has to remember that a significant proportion of new businesses fail within a year, so there will be a flow out of self-employment too. Table A.4 shows that 7.9% of new VAT registered businesses started in 2002 had failed in the first 12 months of trading according to the DTI, and around 30% had failed within the first 3 years. This means that the flow into self-employment must be high in order for the self-employment rate to even remain stable.

In contrast, Chart A.5 shows that the rate of transition of unemployed workers into self-employment falls during periods of economic expansion. For example, just 1.4% of self-employed workers in 2006 had been unemployed in 2005, but the proportion was 3.1% in 1993, when the unemployment rate was at its previous peak. Chart A.6 shows the transition from out of the labor force (OLF), which is uncorrelated with the unemployment rate over the long run.

The self-employment rate is clearly a function of both "push" and "pull" factors, which are related in opposite ways to measures of the economic cycle. It would therefore appear that the two effects cancel each other out to a degree over long periods and cause the self-employment rate to be uncorrelated with the economic cycle. However, it is also the case that other factors are more likely to dominate the decision to become self-employed. During the 1980s and early 1990s, self-employment was stimulated in the UK through changes in: industrial composition, stemming from shifts in relative demand; technological advancements; government policy; and financial markets. We now look at these in turn.

2.1 Industrial Composition

Probably most importantly, the industrial composition of the UK economy started to change. The contribution from service sector industries to total GVA rose from 57% in 1985, to 66% in 1995 (Chart A.7). In contrast, the contribution from manufacturing firms fell by 4pp over the same period, to 22%. Robson (1998) finds that self-employment rates across UK regions are highest in those regions in which "a relatively high proportion of GDP is accounted for by certain industries in which the [financial] barriers to self-employment tend to be relatively low." Consequently, the transition to a predominantly service orientated economy appears to have opened up new opportunities for entrepreneurs.

2.2   Financial Deregulation

The financial hurdles were further eroded by the liberalization of banking rules in the 1980s and the subsequent appreciation of house prices (Chart A.8). Robson (1998) argues that the major source of loan collateral for start-ups in the UK is the equity provided by owner occupied housing. Thus, rising house prices enable liquidity constrained, nascent entrepreneurs to start a business. The annual, nominal[5] rate of house price inflation was positive throughout the 1980s, averaging 12.3%, according to the *Nationwide* index. Indeed, the average UK house price rose 170% between 1980 and 1989. And the home-ownership rate, propelled by the sale of council houses following the 1980 Housing Act and introduction of the Right-to-Buy scheme, rose from 57.6% in 1981 to 65.2% in 1989.[6] Black et al. (1996), for example, found that a 10% rise in the value of unreleased net housing equity increases the number of new firm VAT registrations by some 5%. Cowling and Mitchell (1997) estimate that a 10% rise in housing wealth increases the proportion of the workforce in self-employment by 3%. Over the 1980s, the number of self-employed workers rose by 1,327,000, or 60.2%.

2.3   Government Policies

Financial liberalization *supported* the growth in self-employment, but other government policies were introduced during the 1980s that were specifically aimed at encouraging more workers to become self-

---

[5] The real rate of annual house price inflation was positive from 1983 onwards.
[6] Depart for Communities and Local Government, housing Live Table 101, http://www.communities.gov.uk/index.asp?id=1156006.

employed. Local Enterprise Agencies (LEAs), for example, were created in 1978, to encourage the formation and growth of small firms by providing grants, advice, and training to unemployed workers. The agencies originated as a partnership response from business and local councils to high levels of unemployment and the demise of large sections of manufacturing, particularly in the industrial Midlands and the North, but their work continues today across the UK. These were followed in 1981 by the Loan Guarantee Scheme (LGS), through which the government acts as the guarantor on private sector loans to small and "young" businesses. Loans are made to firms or individuals unable to obtain conventional finance because of a lack of track record or security. The guarantee generally covers 70% of the outstanding loan. This rises to 85% for established businesses trading for two years or more. Loans can be for amounts between £5,000 and £100,000 (£250,000 for established businesses) and over a period of 2–10 years. Data are not available prior to 1995, but in the decade since, 46,531 loans were granted worth about £2 billion. Of these, about a third went to start-ups. Table A.5 shows that of the period total, around a third of firms (14,700) defaulted on their loan.

The Enterprise Allowance Scheme (EAS) ran from 1983 to 1991, paying self-employed workers a supplementary weekly income (of around £40 a week) for up to 12 months. In theory, this scheme compensated workers for a loss of unemployment benefit. Only the very short-term unemployed, those unemployed for less than 13 weeks (although this was later reduced), were excluded from the programme. There were criticisms that the EAS potentially created displacement (occurring when subsidized businesses took output and employment from non-subsidized firms) and "deadweight loss" effects (arising when a subsidy was paid to a firm that would have been set up anyway in the absence of the scheme). Nevertheless, Campbell and Daly (1992) estimate that following implementation, one in eight of those that became self-employed during the late 1980s were supported into employment through this scheme. It is apparent from Table A.3 that in the 12 months following the scheme's introduction self-employment rose by 266k, the largest recorded annual increase of the past 40 years.

2.4   Tax System

The decision to become, and remain, self-employed can also be affected by the tax system. The methods for computing tax between employees and self-employed workers vary significantly in the UK (see Freedman (2001) for a comprehensive discussion). Freedman (2001) argues that attempts to evade the payment of tax in the construction sector influenced movements in self-employment numbers over the late 1980s and 1990s. Under the original rules of the CIS, which is the Inland Revenue's taxation system for the construction industry, employers had an incentive to treat employees as self-employed workers in order to avoid paying National Insurance Contributions, nor provide benefits, training or observe employment protection laws. The Inland Revenue took steps to revise the CIS in 1995 by introducing mandatory registration cards for all subcontractors. Without the card, a subcontractor is treated as an employee. With the card, the subcontractor is paid under deduction of tax and treated as self-employed. Freedman records that 700,000 construction industry workers were treated as self-employed in 1986. But between 1995 and 1997, 200,000 construction workers reclassified themselves as employees, which can more than explain the reduction in self-employment over the period (−100k). Table A.6 records a 12pp fall in the construction sector self-employment *rate* between 1995 and 2000 using LFS data, while most other sectors (the exception being agriculture) recorded more modest declines, or small increases. The years 2000–2005 show an increase in the self-employment share of construction workers. Table A.7 shows the changes in the industry distribution of the self-employed. The declining importance of construction in terms of its share from 1995 to 2000 is striking, as is its increased importance subsequently, alongside increases in Real Estate, Renting, and Business Activities.

Changes in the tax system can also have large, and sometimes unexpected, ramifications for the numbers of workers who choose to become self-employed. For instance, the UK government abolished corporation tax on the first £10,000 of company profits in April 2002, and also allowed directors of small companies to save income tax by taking their salaries as profits. This may have stimulated some already self-employed workers to incorporate in order to avoid paying income tax and national insurance contributions. But the changes probably also contributed to an increase in the number of employees who became self-employed; the number of self-employed workers increased by 10.1% between 2002Q1 and 2003Q4, according to the LFS. This increase is reflected in a rise in the proportion of self-employed workers who had been employees a year earlier. Table A.8 shows that the flows from employment into self-employment, while volatile, peaked in 2002–2003. The largest increase in self-employment (around half) during 2002–2003 came in the Banking, Finance, and Insurance sectors and was dominated by the 35–49 age group, although there were also large increases in the 50–64/59 and 65/60 and over age groups. The rise seems consistent with media stories about City job losses leading to people moving into self-employment (Lindsay and Macaulay (2004)). In any case, the government re-considered its position following the increase in incorporations and decided to tax distributed profits at 19% in 2004, thus reducing the incentives for workers to turn to self-employment. Following this tax change, the flows from employment into self-employment declined.

2.5 Price of Investment Goods

An additional exogenous stimulus to self-employment growth over the past few decades has been a steady decline in the price of investment goods, particularly information, communication, and technology (ICT) products, relative to other goods (Chart A.9). Such a decline can be explained by an increase in technological progress in the development of these goods in comparison with other sectors (Bakhshi and Thompson, 2002). These price falls will have increased the relative rates of return from self-employment, making independence more attractive (Blau, 1987; Acs et al., 1994).

Over the past couple of years there has been a substantial growth in the numbers of self employed as well as in the self-employment rate. The data in Table 2.3 are taken from Table A.3 of Labour Market Statistics First Release, ONS April 2007. Total employment also includes small numbers of unpaid family workers and those on Government schemes. The numbers of self-employed over the period Dec–Feb 2005–2007 increased by 187,000, representing 64.0% of the

Table 2.3

	Total employment ('000s)	Employees ('000s)	Others ('000s)	Self-employed ('000s) (rate)
Dec–Feb 2005	28,690	24,824	230	3,636 (12.67%)
Dec–Feb 2006	28,835	24,924	181	3,730 (12.94%)
Mar–May 2006	28,895	25,002	182	3,711 (12.84%)
Jun–Aug 2006	29,015	25,077	194	3,743 (12.90%)
Sep–Nov 2006	29,029	25,025	211	3,793 (13.07%)
Dec–Feb 2007	28,982	24,957	203	3,823 (13.19%)
2 year change	+292	+133	−27	+187

total growth of employment of 292,000 over the period.[7] Moreover, only 37.6% of the additional employee jobs were full-time compared with 61.8% of self-employed jobs. In addition, over the most recent quarter, December 2006–February 2007, the number of employees fell by 68,000 while the number of self-employed *grew* by 30,000. What explains this increase?

Early analysis of LFS data for the period 2004–2006 suggests little if any change in the distribution of the self-employed by industry (Table A.7) or by occupation or region.[8] However, there have been

---

[7] In Table 2.3, "others" includes unpaid family workers and those on Government supported training and employment programmes.

[8] The distribution of the self-employed by region of residence is as follows:

	2001–2003	2004–2006
Tyne & Wear	1.02	1.02
Rest of Northern region	2.40	2.68
South Yorkshire	1.54	1.56
West Yorkshire	2.81	2.90
Rest of Yorks & Humberside	2.63	2.76
East Midlands	6.71	6.91
East Anglia	4.15	3.89
Inner London	6.03	5.93
Outer London	8.58	9.16
Rest of South East	22.64	22.52
South West	10.32	9.71
West Midlands (met county)	3.03	3.20
Rest of West Midlands	4.51	4.73
Greater Manchester	3.43	3.53
Merseyside	1.44	1.46
Rest of North West	3.91	3.72
Wales	4.79	4.47
Strathclyde	2.51	2.40
Rest of Scotland	4.49	4.22
Northern Ireland	3.07	3.24

Table 2.4

	Age	% male	% immigrant	# observations
2001	45.30	73.31	10.26	29,929
2002	45.31	73.10	10.29	29,839
2003	45.40	72.93	10.83	30,486
2004	45.45	73.36	11.10	29,194
2005	45.71	73.13	11.12	29,219
2006	45.84	72.26	12.48	29,137

increases in the proportion of the self-employed that are (a) immigrants, (b) females. At the same time there have been increases in the age of the self-employed and a decline in the hours worked over this period. Chart A.10 shows changes in the transition rates into and out of self-employment since 1995 for those of working age using matched data from the LFS. Data are only available from the ONS to do this matching for those of working age. There is little evidence of much change in the transition rates over time. The most pronounced change has been a small increase in the flow into self-employment from inactivity.

Chart A.11 shows that self-employment rates have remained roughly constant over time at all ages except for those above retirement age, which continues to rise for both men and women. As a result the average age of the self-employed continues to rise. In Table 2.4, we present the (weighted) age, proportion male and proportion immigrant of the self-employed between 2001 and 2006 from the LFS.

Data are available in the Spring quarter of each year of the LFS from the variables *oycirc* and *oystat*, which report the individual's labor market status and whether they were self-employed or not a year earlier and is not restricted to those of working age. These enable us to calculate transition probabilities for all ages (as in Table A.8 and Charts A.4–A.6). The labor market status in year $t - 1$ for those who were self-employed in year t are reported in Table 2.5. It is apparent that the outflow rate from self-employment has slowed while the inflow rate from OLF has increased alongside a decline in the inflow rate from being an employee.

It is also feasible to use these data to identify which industries the new self-employed move into. Here we define the new self-employed as individuals who were self-employed in period t, but not self-employed

Table 2.5

	2001–2003 (n = 20,656)	2004–2006 (n = 19,608)
Self-employed	86.69	87.12
Employee	9.26	8.65
Unemployed	1.43	1.25
OLF	2.62	2.99

Table 2.6

	2001–2003	2004–2006
Agriculture, hunting & forestry	2.99	3.25
Fishing	0.20	0.10
Mining, quarrying	0.22	0.12
Manufacturing	6.95	6.96
Electricity gas & water supply	0.30	0.28
Construction	18.40	19.30
Wholesale, retail & motor trade	11.45	11.44
Hotels & restaurants	3.95	2.57
Transport, storage & communication	7.94	6.48
Financial intermediation	1.99	1.96
Real estate, renting & business activities	20.03	18.94
Public administration & defence	0.87	1.04
Education	3.80	3.81
Health & social work	7.44	7.75
Other community, social & personal	9.99	13.37
Private households with employed persons	3.42	2.59
Extra-territorial organizations	0.03	0.04
N	2,950	2,749

in $t - 1$. Table 2.6 shows the industry distribution of the changers (%). The biggest change is the increase in the proportion working in Other Community, Social and Personal.

At this time it is by no means obvious *why* the self-employment rate has increased. In part it is because of increased immigration alongside moves to self-employment from those who had previously been OLF. It does not appear that the most recent increase in self-employment has been the result of changes in regulation, tax changes or changes in the minimum wage (Blanchflower et al. 2007a, 2007b). However, we do believe that moving house prices are a significant explanatory factor through their ability to ease credit constraints (see Section 6).

3

Self-Employment and Earnings

We make use of data from the Family Resources Survey (FRS) and the Survey of Personal Incomes (SPI) conducted by HMRC to compare the earnings of the self-employed with those of employees, as the LFS does not ask respondents who classify themselves as being self-employed about their labor income(s). The earnings distributions for the self-employed and employees are very different. Median incomes are lower for the self-employed than for employees, but the self-employed distribution has a longer right-hand tail, so somebody 90% up the self-employment earnings distribution has higher earnings than an employee at the 90th percentile of the wage and salary distribution. For example, the median gross weekly income from self-employment in 2005 was £249 (£12,948 annually), according to the FRS. This compares with £333 per week (£17,316 annually) for employees (Chart A.12a). The lower weekly income for self-employed workers partly reflects the fact that 6.9% of self-employed workers actually earned nothing, or lost money as a result of their occupation in 2005. Excluding these workers causes the median gross weekly wage rate to rise to £276 (a sixth less than employed workers).

The relative success of those at the top end of the self-employed income distribution is particularly striking if one looks at means rather than medians; the pay levels of the two groups are almost identical on this measure (Chart A.12b). This indicates that there are significant returns available for successful entrepreneurs. But the fact that more than 80% of self-employed workers earn less than employees "is noteworthy considering the age distribution of the self-employed is older than that of employees (Weir, 2003)."

HMRC collects data on individuals' incomes, principally for tax modeling and forecasting purposes. A sample of this data is made available in the form of the SPI, which provides the most comprehensive and accurate official source of data on personal incomes in the UK. The dataset contains a range of variables related to taxable personal incomes arising from employment, self-employment, pensions, benefits, property, savings and investments and other income sources. Also included are variables related to allowances, deductions and tax relief that people may be due. A limitation of the data, however, is that a continuous time series is only available from 1999/2000. The SPI is carried out annually.[1] Data are collected from three HMRC operational IT systems, which are as follows:

(1) COP: this covers all employees and occupational or personal pension recipients with a PAYE record;

(2) CESA: this covers the self assessment (SA) population; those with self-employment, rent or untaxed investment income, directors and other people with complex tax affairs or high incomes. Some people have both a COP and CESA record.

(3) Claims: this covers people without COP or CESA records who have had too much tax deducted at source and claim repayment.

HMRC has kindly supplied data to us on employee and self-employee income distributions from the SPI, for the financial years 1999/2000–2003/2004. The distributions are banded, with lower limit thresholds ranging from zero (for self-employees) to £100,000+. The

---

[1] The approximate sample sizes for recent survey years are as follows: 1999/2000, $n = 150,000$; 2000/2001, $n = 200,000$; 2001/2002, $n = 300,000$; 2002/2003, $n = 400,000$; 2003/2004, $n = 400,000$.

Table 3.1

Lower limit of employment income	Employees			Self-employed		
	Amounts (£m)	Numbers (000's)	Cumulative (%)	Amounts (£m)	Numbers (000's)	Cumulative (%)
0				–	510	11.2
£1	22	84	0.4	39	161	14.8
£500	67	91	0.8	112	153	18.1
£1,000	212	141	1.5	387	263	23.9
£2,000	400	160	2.2	601	242	29.2
£3,000	641	182	3.1	879	251	34.7
£4,000	2,838	609	5.9	1,448	323	41.9
£5,000	13,688	2,196	16.3	3,003	484	52.5
£7,500	18,142	2,074	26.0	3,133	360	60.4
£10,000	51,838	4,153	45.5	6,749	548	72.4
£15,000	62,191	3,578	62.3	6,432	372	80.6
£20,000	109,247	4,473	83.3	10,023	414	89.7
£30,000	95,336	2,582	95.4	9,624257		95.4
£50,000	51,840	788	99.1	9,675	140	98.5
£100,000	39,643	195	100.0	15,647	70	100
Total	£446,000	21,300		£67,752	4,547	

data presented in Table 3.1 for 2003/2004 indicate that 4.0 million individuals earned some income from self-employment – while another half a million self-employed reported no positive income. This compares with 3.63 million self-reported self-employed in the LFS for the same period. The difference between the two numbers reflects the fact that some individuals have more than one job. Total earnings from self-employment are recorded at £67,750 million in 2003/2004, compared with £446,000 million for employees. Earnings from self-employment therefore represented 13.19% of the combined total of earnings.

There is evidence then, that on average, the self-employed are paid less than employees. Hamilton (2000) finds similar evidence in the US and argues that this arises in part because of the non-pecuniary benefits of "being your own boss" (2000, p. 628). Similarly, Taylor (1996), using data for the UK from the British Household Panel Study for the Autumn of 1991, found that the self-employed had lower hourly earnings than employees (1996, Appendix).[2] Weir (2003), using data from the 2001/2002 FRS, found that the first four-fifths of self-employed workers in the income distribution earn less than the first four-fifths

---

[2] £8.20 and £9.71 per hour, respectively (Taylor, 1996).

of employees, but the highest one-fifth earned more than employees. Updating this analysis indicates little change in the distribution over the past decade. Charts A.13a & A.13b provide income distributions for 2003/2004 and 1994/1995, respectively, using data from the FRS. These results are broadly supported by data from HMRC with data for 2003/2004 and 1999/2000 from the SPI (Charts A.14a & A.14b), although the proportion of self-employed workers earning more than employees is slightly smaller.

One problem with these earnings measures will be the extent to which the self-employed under-report their income because they inappropriately charge some of their income to expenses. There is also the possibility that work is paid for "under the table" – self-employment allows more opportunities to work in the black economy.[3] It is very difficult to obtain quantitative estimates for such illegal activities. Lyssiotou et al. (2004) estimate the size of the black economy by estimating the extent to which self-employment income is under-reported in the UK, using data from the 1993 Family Expenditure Survey. The idea is to use data on consumption to obtain an idea of the degree of under-reporting. Their empirical analysis suggests that the size of the self-employment related black economy in the UK amounts to 10.6% of GDP. They also found that households with a head in a blue collar self-employment occupation under-report more than households with a head in a white collar self-employment occupation.

We can appreciate the significant returns available to the most successful entrepreneurs based in Britain by looking at the Sunday Times Rich List. The list, which is compiled annually, records estimates of the minimum identifiable wealth of Britain's 1,000 richest people or families.[4] The results measure identifiable wealth, whether land, property, racehorses, art or significant shares in publicly quoted companies. Personal bank accounts are excluded – as access is not permitted. The most recent valuations available at the time of writing were carried out

---

[3] Indeed, Fairlie (2002) finds that a specific group of people who worked in the black economy – drug dealers – were more likely to be self-employed in the real economy later, presumably because they understood risk taking.

[4] The actual size of their fortunes may be much larger than the figures estimated by the Sunday Times.

at the beginning of January 2007.[5] The results show that the richest entrepreneur in Britain (and 7th in the world) was Lakshmi Mittal, worth £19,250 million. The 1,000th richest person had an estimated personal fortune of £70 million. Clearly the returns for the most successful self-employed far exceed the highest paid employees – although some on the list have made a significant proportion of their wealth as city traders. The wealthiest trader in the 2007 list, which we might take to be the wealthiest employee in Britain, was Michael Sherwood, worth an estimated £225 million (319th).

Of those in the 2007 list, 1,028 were men and just 92 were women – the number is higher than 1,000 because some entries are couples or families. The eldest entrant was aged 94, while the youngest was 25. There are a total of 774 self-made millionaires, while the rest inherited their wealth. A fifth of the most wealthy made their fortunes in land and property. The breakdown by industry corresponds closely with our previous analysis of the LFS (Table 3.2).

Over half of the entrants live, or have their primary interests centred in London (41%) or the south east (12%), again similar to our results from the LFS (see Table 3.3).

Table 3.2

Industry	Number
Land and property	221
Banking, insurance, stockbroking and finance	155
Industry, engineering, metal bashing, steel making	106
Retailing (not food)	71
Construction, house building	64
Hotels, leisure, health and fitness, sport	62
Computers, software, Internet, telecoms, mobile phones	60
Food retailing, food production, drink	59
Media, television and films, publishing, novels	55
Music	36
Business services, recruitment, office support	31
Car sales, wholesaling and distribution	27
Pharmaceuticals, nursing homes, health care	27
Transport	26

---

[5] For more details, see http://business.timesonline.co.uk/tol/business/specials/rich_list/article1716427.ece.

Table 3.3

Region	Number of entries
London	411
South East	123
North West	68
Scotland	65
East Midlands	40
Yorkshire	39
West Midlands	37
South West	36
East Anglia	26
Wales	25
North East	16
Ireland	42
Channels Isles, Isle of Man	27
Overseas	51

Table 3.4

	Name	Worth	Industry
1	Lakshmi Mittal and family	£19,250m	Steel
2	Roman Abramovich	£10,800m	Oil and industry
3	The Duke of Westminster	£7,000m	Property
4	Sri and Gopi Hinduja	£6,200m	Industry and finance
5	David Khalili	£5,800m	Art and property
6	Hans Rausing and family	£5,400m	Packaging
7	Sir Philip and Lady Green	£4,900m	Retailing
8	John Fredriksen	£3,500m	Shipping
9	David and Simon Reuben	£3,490m	Metals and property
10	Jim Ratcliffe	£3,300m	Chemicals
11	Sir Richard Branson	£3,100m	Transport and mobile phones
12	Charlene and Michel de Carvalho	£3,050m	Inheritance, brewing and banking
13	Sean Quinn and family	£3,050m	Quarrying, property and insurance
14	Simon Halabi	£3,000m	Property, health clubs
15	Kirsten and Jorn Rausing	£2,825m	Inheritance and investments

The top 15 entrants in 2007 are not confined to any particular industry (see Table 3.4).

The average age of the top 15 wealthiest entrants in 2007 was 58. Of those that are self-made billionaires, rather than having inherited their fortunes (as is the case for the Duke of Westminster, Charlene and Michel de Carvalho, and Kirsten and Jorn Rausing), six have a degree-level education and six do not. None of the British born entrants in the top 15 has a degree. We could only find an estimated income figure for Lakshmi Mittal, which was estimated to be £413 million in 2007. But are these characteristics the exception or the rule?

4

Who are the Self-Employed?

Thus far we have explained factors that may exogenously affect individuals' decisions to become self-employed. But what if some workers are more pre-disposed to becoming self-employed than others? It is appropriate at this point to compare the characteristics of the self-employed with those of employees. We do so by examining weighted means from the UK LFS.

4.1 Age

In the LFS, self-employed workers (aged 16+) were on average six years older than their employed counterparts in 2006 (45.8 vs. 39.3, respectively). Chart A.15 illustrates that the age distribution of the self-employed is skewed to the right, compared with that for employees. It seems plausible that younger workers are less likely to have the necessary human capital (experience) to become self-employed. Younger individuals are probably also more likely to be credit constrained, limiting a larger proportion of them from starting a new business. At the other end of the distribution, older workers face retirement, but that is not an issue for the self-employed. Indeed, many retirees (either at state pension age or earlier) may take advantage of the opportunity self-employment brings to remain in the workplace, providing their skills on their own terms. It is probably also fair to say that there is an element of risk in becoming self-employed, and this risk can be minimized if workers have previously ensured financial stability (e.g., mortgage paid off) by working for others.

4.2   Gender, Marital Status and Children

The split between male and female employees is roughly equal (56.6% male). However, the micro-data suggest that the self-employed are predominantly male (80.1% in 2006). This probably reflects the fact that self-employment is more common in industries not usually associated with high levels of female employment, such as construction. It may also be a by-product of the fact that a much higher proportion of women are part-time workers.

The self-employed are more likely to be married than employees (see Table 4.1). The self-employed have more dependent children in their family under the age of 19 (0.79 children) than is the case of employees (0.71).[1] This is consistent with the findings of Broussard et al. (2003) for the US.

Table 4.1

	Employee (%)	Self-employed (%)
Single	36	22
Married	53	65
Separated	3	3
Divorced	8	9
Widowed	1	1

4.3   Industry and Occupation

The self-employed are more likely to work in occupations that are human-capital and labor intensive, such as construction, financial

---

[1] In sweep 13 of the British Household Panel Study of 2003/2004 the (weighted) self-employed also had more children than employees (0.71 and 0.61, respectively), which includes natural children, adopted children, and step children, under the age of 16.

activities or agriculture. Chart A.16 shows that nearly a quarter of self-employed individuals worked in the construction industry in 2006, compared with just 6% of employees. A further 20% worked in finance, real estate, and business activities and almost all agricultural employees – though few in total – were self-employed. In general, we would think that service sector industries are more suited to self-employment as there will typically be lower start-up costs, reducing barriers to entry; although a lack of human capital or qualifications to signal ability (certainly for business activities, such as consultancy) may act as impediments.

4.4   Education

Chart A.17 shows that about a fifth of both employees and self-employed workers had a degree in 2006. Indeed, the distributions of the two sets of workers are very similar in general. The one major difference is the higher proportion of the self-employed with Apprenticeship and craft qualifications (see Table 4.2).

This suggests that the decision to become self-employed is not related to educational attainment, although, as we noted above, it seems to be more related to age and experience. This is quite different from the US where self-employment rates are particularly high among those with higher degrees, especially MBAs (see Blanchflower and Wainwright, 2005). We provide more assessment of the differences in the characteristics of the self-employed between the US and the UK below.

Table 4.2

	Employee (%)	Self-employed (%)
Degree	21	21
Higher education	10	8
Apprenticeship, City and Guild Crafts etc.	24	30
GCSE grades A–C	23	17
Other	12	12
None	9	12
DK	1	1

4.5   Co-workers

The weighted LFS micro-data for 2004–2006 show that three-quarters of the self-employed work alone or in a partnership (see Table 4.3).

This would seem intuitive for business activities and consultancy, where specialist individuals may be employed by larger firms, or agriculture, where a lone individual can use technology to tend many activities. The distribution by industry for those with and without employees is as shown in Table 4.4. The main difference is that the self-employed tend to be sole contractors in construction and have employees in distribution.

When the self-employed do employ others, more than 90% have fewer than 20 employees. This is in stark contrast to the employed, where two-thirds work in firms employing 25 or more workers. Interestingly, the proportion of the self-employed with employees has shown a steady decline over time, corroborating the trend in the VAT registrations data presented earlier (see Table 4.5).

Table 4.3

	Employee	Self-employed
Works alone/with partner	0%	77%
1–10 employees	18%	18%
11–19 employees	9%	2%
20–24 employees	4%	1%
25–49 employees	14%	1%
50–249 employees	23%	1%
250–499 employees	8%	0.1%
500 or more employees	18%	0.2%
Other	6%	0%

Table 4.4

	Works alone	With employees
Agriculture	5%	5%
Energy & water	0%	0%
Manufacturing	6%	8%
Construction	26%	16%
Distribution	12%	28%
Transport	8%	5%
Banking	19%	21%
Public administration	10%	10%
Other services	14%	7%

Table 4.5

	% with employees
1992	29.1
1993	27.7
1994	27.3
1995	26.7
1996	25.7
1997	26.8
1998	26.4
1999	26.4
2000	26.8
2001	26.8
2002	24.9
2003	24.0
2004	24.1
2005	23.2
2006	22.9

The fact that most self-employed firms are small (in terms of employment) is suggestive of a degree of flexibility.

4.6 Hours

The self-employed tend to work longer hours than employees. On average, the self-employed worked 40 hours per week in 2006, compared with only 34 hours for employees (Chart A.18). However, the self-employed are only marginally less likely than employees to say that they are part-timers. For example, the latest figures available at the time of writing are for December 2006–February 2007 and show that 25.7% of employees were part-time compared with 23.6% of the self-employed. Moreover, if the self-employed report that they are part-time they actually work fewer usual hours than employees (17.3 and 18.1 per week, respectively) whereas the reverse is the case for those who report being full-timers (46.3 and 39.3 hours, respectively).

4.7 Region

There is considerable variation by region in self-employment rates. In 2006, using region of work to define location, self-employment rates ranged from under 8% in Tyne and Wear to just under 19% in Outer London (see Table 4.6).

Table 4.6

Tyne & Wear	7.8
Rest northern region	12.3
South Yorkshire	10.9
West Yorkshire	11.1
Rest Yorks. & Humberside	11.7
East Midlands	11.9
East Anglia	13.4
Central London	8.0
Inner London	18.3
Outer London	18.8
Rest of South East	14.5
South West	13.5
West Midlands Metropolitan	10.0
Rest West Midlands	14.0
Greater Manchester	11.6
Merseyside	9.0
Rest NW	12.2
Wales	12.9
Strathclyde	8.6
Rest of Scotland	11.4
Northern Ireland	15.8

4.8   Immigrants

There are differences in self-employment rates by race. In 2006, in the UK, the rate for whites was 13.0% compared with 14.6% for Asians, 8.5% for blacks, and 17.1% for Chinese. The self-employment rate of immigrants is generally higher than that of the indigenous population. Clark and Drinkwater (2000), in their study of self-employment among ethnic minorities in England and Wales, found that minorities who live in areas which have a high percentage of their own group are *less* likely to be self-employed. They found that those with poor language skills (typically more recent immigrants) had lower self-employment probabilities. Borooah and Hart (1999) used data from the British 1991 Census to examine why so many Indians, but so few black Caribbeans in Britain are self-employed? Over 20% of economically active Indian males, but only 8% of economically active black Caribbean males, were self-employed. The reluctance of black men to become self-employed was, as this study suggested, because of two factors. First, they were, relative to whites and Indians, "ethnically disinclined" to enter business – this stunted their desire to be self-employed. Second, they did not possess, relative to whites and Indians, the attributes that were positively related to entering business – this impaired their ability to be self-employed. The authors estimated that 58% of the observed lack (relative to Indians) of self-employed black males was because of ethnic disinclination and 42% was a result of attribute disadvantage. Of course this result begs the question of why Caribbean men were disinclined to be self-employed. Clark and Drinkwater (2000) also reported that, based on the 1991 Census of Population, self-employment rates for blacks in England and Wales were 5.8% compared with 26.6% for Chinese and 12.3% for whites and 14.6% for non-whites.[2]

Column 1 of Table A.9 presents data from the LFS of 2004–2006, which contain data on 633,161 workers and shows that the (weighted) self-employment rate for the UK born was 12.5% compared with 14.5% for immigrants and 12.7% overall. The data file is restricted to those aged 16–70. The table also suggests that there is considerable variation in self-employment rates by the immigrants' country of birth. Self-employment rates were highest among those born in Romania (44%), Iran (32%), Thailand (32%), Pakistan (31%) and Turkey (27%) and lowest for those born in the Philippines (3%), Slovakia (3%) and Finland (1%). Self-employment rates tend to be lower for more recent immigrants, in part, for the very obvious reason, that they tend to be younger. For example, average self-employment rates and average age based on number of years in the UK for immigrants is shown in Table 4.7 (LFS 2004–2006):

Table 4.7

	Self-employment rate	Average age
< 2 years	4.9%	29.5
< 5 years	7.1%	30.9
5–9 years	13.0%	33.8
10–19 years	15.9%	37.2
≥ 20 years	28.0%	40.4

---

[2] Using data from the Fourth National Survey of Ethnic Minorities conducted in 1993/1994. Clark and Drinkwater (2000) found self-employment rates to be especially high, among both men and women, for Pakistanis, Indians, and African Asians.

In the second column of Table A.9 we present equivalent evidence on self-employment rates by country of birth for the US using data for 2,552,483 workers from the Basic Monthly files of the Current Population Survey. Here we define self-employment to include both the unincorporated and the incorporated self-employed. In the official statistics the self-employment rate only includes the unincorporated, although their earnings are not included in wage and salary measures.[3] We only present evidence for countries where there are matched pairs – these exclusions are not significant. In the US, the self-employment rate of immigrants (10.1%) is marginally less than that of the indigenous population (10.6%). The self-employment rate of the UK born in the US (12.8%) is virtually identical to the rate in the UK as a whole (12.7%). In contrast the self-employment rates, of those born in the US who reside in the UK, (17.6%) is higher than in the US (10.6%). Interestingly, there is no correlation between the self employment rates across the two countries.

4.9   Self-Employed Second Jobs

The LFS data indicate that a number of individuals who are employees also work self-employed in a second job. It turns out that this is a particularly important phenomenon in the public sector, especially among academics and health professionals, including therapists. It is especially high for those with higher degrees. Overall, 0.9% of employees in their main job had a second job that was self-employed: the rate was 0.6% in the private sector and 1.5% in the public (see Table 4.8).

4.10   Happiness, Life and Job Satisfaction

The self-employed are generally more satisfied with their jobs than employees (Blanchflower and Oswald, 1998; Blanchflower, 2004; Green and Tsitsianis, 2005). In an important paper, Frey and Benz (2002) examine job satisfaction data for the UK, Germany, and Switzerland and find evidence that the self-employed are more satisfied at work than

---

[3] See, for example, Table 591 of the 2007 Statistical Abstract of the US, www.census. gov/compendia/statab/tables/07s0591.xls.

Table 4.8

Private sector	0.6%
Public sector	1.5%
Public company, PLC	0.7%
Nationalized industry	0.6%
Central Govt., Civil Service	0.9%
Local Govt. or council (inc police etc.)	1.4%
University, etc.	3.0%
Health authority or NHS trust	1.8%
Charity, voluntary orgn. etc.	2.5%
Armed forces	0.3%
Other public organization	1.0%
UK	0.9%

employees. What is impressive about this paper is that the authors have panel data over a number of years on the same individuals for both the UK (1991–1999) and Germany (1984–2000) and show that this result remains even in the presence of people specific fixed effects. There is also some recent evidence from Finland suggesting that the self-employed are less risk averse than employees. Ekelund et al. (2005) used data from the 1966 Northern Finnish Birth Cohort Study. Unfortunately the measure of risk-aversion is a contemporaneous one so it is difficult to determine causality.

The self-employed seem to like their jobs despite the fact that their work is not easy. The self-employed report that they (a) work under a lot of pressure, (b) find their work stressful, (c) come home from work exhausted, (d) are constantly under strain, (e) lose sleep over worry, (f) place more weight on work than they do on leisure, but (g) are especially likely to say they have control over their lives (Blanchflower, 2004).

The self-employed in the UK also tend to report relatively high levels of happiness and life satisfaction (Blanchflower, 2004; Blanchflower and Oswald, 2004) and job satisfaction (Taylor, 2004; Green and Tsitsianis, 2005). To illustrate, the European Quality of Life Survey of 2003 asked respondents for their happiness, life satisfaction, and job satisfaction on a scale of 1–10, with 10 being highest. The weighted average job satisfaction score for the UK was 8.31 for the self-employed and 7.22 for employees. The weighted scores for life satisfaction and happiness for the UK in 2003 are shown in Table 4.9.

Table 4.9

	Life satisfaction ($n = 980$)	Happiness ($n = 984$)
Self-employed	7.7	8.0
Employee	7.4	7.9
Homemaker	6.9	7.6
Unemployed	6.5	6.7
Retired	7.5	7.9
Student	7.7	8.1

Results are similar in the British Household Panel Study Sweep 13 taken primarily during 2004 with around 8% of responses in 2005. Levels of overall job satisfaction – based on a scale of 1 through 7 – were 5.7 for the self-employed and 5.4 for employees. In addition the self-employed were also less satisfied with their job security (5.0 and 5.5) and their hours (5.0 and 5.3). Analogously the self-employed scored 5.4 and employees 5.2 when asked if they were satisfied with their life overall, once again on a scale of 1–7. The self-employed in the UK score highly on job satisfaction, life satisfaction, and happiness.

4.11   Independence

The self-employed are especially likely to report that they value their independence. Benz and Frey (2003) examined data on 23 countries from the International Social Survey Programme (ISSP). They conclude that the self-employed are more satisfied with their jobs because they enjoy "greater autonomy and independence." In a recent paper Hundley (2001) provides results for the US which, are similar to those of Benz and Frey. His main findings are that the self-employed are more satisfied because their work provides more autonomy, flexibility and skill utilization and greater job security. In the Flash Eurobarometer Survey #160 conducted in April 2004 individuals in EU member countries were asked "suppose you could choose between different kinds of jobs, which one would you prefer – being an employee or self-employed?." On average 47.1% said they would prefer to be self-employed. The individuals who said they were self-employed were asked to give reasons why and were allowed to provide multiple answers. The major reason by far was "personal independence/self-

fulfilment/interesting tasks." On average across these countries, 70%
gave this answer – the next highest response was better income
prospects (23%). Responses by country on independence are in column 1 below ($n = 9,358$). Only in the US did fewer than half of the
respondents give this answer, but a further 61% in the US said "no
need to adapt to an environment." These proportions by country are
in the second column of Table 4.10

The self-employed report that they like another aspect of independence, the flexibility the job brings and the fact that they can pick
their schedule (Hyytinen and Ruuskanen, 2007). However, the self-
employed are especially likely to report being stressed (Blanchflower,
2004). Respondents in the 14th sweep of the BHPS were asked "Do you

Table 4.10

	Independence (%)	No need to adapt (%)
Austria	76	19
Belgium	69	10
Cyprus	69	11
Czech Republic	81	55
Denmark	83	6
Estonia	84	7
Finland	79	22
France	86	12
Germany	85	22
Greece	80	30
Hungary	65	26
Iceland	67	7
Ireland	84	4
Italy	80	18
Latvia	61	43
Lichtenstein	80	28
Lithuania	64	26
Luxembourg	59	19
Malta	80	8
Netherlands	72	30
Norway	77	14
Poland	66	10
Portugal	62	11
Slovakia	64	28
Slovenia	73	5
Spain	66	7
Sweden	75	9
UK	81	9
USA	21	61

Table 4.11

	Employee (%)	Self-employed (%)
Never	42.6	35.1
Occasionally	31.3	29.4
Some of the time	16.9	22.6
Much of the time	4.8	6.9
Most of the time	3.1	3.8
All of the time	1.3	2.2

worry about job problems after work?" Weighted responses are shown in Table 4.11.

The self-employed were more likely than employees to worry about job problems after work.

5

Econometric Analysis of the Probability of a Randomly Selected Worker being Self-Employed

Given the differences that exist in the characteristics of the self-employed in terms of their location, occupation, industry, schooling, age, and gender it is appropriate to examine the extent to which there have been changes over time, *holding constant these characteristics*, in a regression framework. There is a growing body of research that has examined the probability that a randomly sampled worker is self-employed (see Blanchflower 2000, 2004 for a summary). The main results from this work are as follows. Self-employment is higher among men than women; among older workers than younger workers. It is also especially high among some immigrant groups, such as Asians. It does vary by location, being especially high in construction occupations, agriculture and retailing. These results are updated below.

Tables A.10 and A.11 report the results of estimating the probability of a randomly selected worker being self-employed. The dependent variable is set to one if self-employed, zero if an employee; the estimation procedure is dprobit in STATA.[1] Data used are from

---

[1] The *dprobit* procedure in STATA fits maximum-likelihood probit models and is an alternative to probit. Rather than reporting the coefficients, dprobit reports the marginal effect, that is the change in the probability for an infinitesimal change in each independent,

the LFS and in Table A.10 cover the period from January 1994 to December 1996, while Table A.11 performs an equivalent exercise 10 years later for January 2004 to December 2006. In the first period, the mean self-employment rate in our data was 13.7% compared with 12.7% in the subsequent period. Where feasible identical controls are included; the major exception is occupation because of changes in the classification system used by the ONS in 2000. Controls in column 1 include age and its square; a gender dummy; four race dummies and six schooling dummies. As we move across the columns controls are added – an immigrant dummy in column 2; region of residence and industry dummies in column 3 and occupation dummies in column 4. Interestingly, the patterns in the means isolated above are robust in the regressions.

The main findings are as follows:

(1) The probability of self-employment rises non-linearly with age and reaches a maximum at age 63.8 in column 1 of Table A.10 and at age 70 in column 4. In column 1 of Table A.11, for the later period the maximum was 76.7 compared with 73.0 in column 4. The positive sign on the age variable and the negative sign on the age squared term permits the calculation of these maxima.

(2) The probability of self-employment is higher for men, whites, Asians and immigrants generally, as well as for those with A-levels or equivalent, of which over half are individuals with trade apprenticeships (5.5%) or City & Guilds Advanced Craft Qualifications (45.3%). Probabilities are also high in the South West and London as well as in Agriculture and Construction. Occupations with high self-employment rates include Health Professionals; Construction Trades; Hairdressers; Artistic and Sports Occupations and Agricultural Occupations.

---

continuous variable and, by default, reports the discrete change in the probability for dummy variables.

(3) The probability of self-employment is relatively low for blacks and those with Higher Education qualifications, which primarily include NVQ level 4 and teaching qualifications. It is also low in Distribution and Manufacturing and, of course, in the Public Sector. *Ceteris paribus* rates were lowest in Tyne and Wear in both periods.

(4) It is apparent that the patterns that emerge in Table A.11 for 2004–2006 are very similar to those for the period 1994–1996. The age maximum increased over time, as noted above, but the gender, education and race gaps were broadly unchanged.

Table A.12 presents the results of estimating a further dprobit modeling the probability that an employee in their main job will have a *second job* where they are self-employed. So the dependent variable is one if an employee in the first job and self-employed in the second zero otherwise. All those reporting being self-employed in their first job are omitted. Probabilities are higher for men, whites and rise with age reaching a maximum over the age 54 in column 3. They are especially high in London and East Anglia. As noted earlier, self-employed second jobs are especially important for people with higher degrees and teaching qualifications and are particularly important in universities. If we count these individuals into the self-employment count they add nearly a percentage point (mean $= 0.87\%$).

How do the characteristics of the self-employed in the UK compare with those in the US? As background, Table A.13 provides details of the distribution of incorporated and unincorporated self-employment and wage and salary employment by gender, race and whether foreign born for the US in 2005.[2] There were approximately twice as many unincorporated self-employed than incorporated – 10 and a half million and 5 and a quarter million, respectively. The incidence of self-employment is highest in middle age and is higher among men. In comparison with wage and salary work, minori-

---

[2] Note that the unincorporated self-employment rate is actually constructed as in Table A.9 as the proportion of the unincorporated self-employed over total workers, which in 2005 was 7.4%.

ties are under-represented in self-employment. For example, 11.5% of wage and salary workers are black compared with 6.3% of unincorporated and 3.7% of incorporated self-employed and similarly for the foreign born. In contrast, Asians have a higher representation in incorporated self-employment than they do in wage and salary work.

Table A.14 presents econometric evidence for the US, using data from the Basic Monthly files of the Current Population Survey (BMCPS) comparable to that for the UK in Table A.11, again for 2004–2006. The US sample size is four times larger at over two and a half million workers. The dependent variable is defined in the same way as in Tables A.10 and A.11, set to one if self-employed and zero if an employee. As in Table A.9, the self-employed includes both the incorporated and unincorporated (Blanchflower and Wainwright, 2005).

It is necessary, however, to make an adjustment in the various regressions we report because there are repeat observations of individuals and households in the Current Population Survey. This has the effect of biasing downwards the size of the standard errors and biasing upwards the *t*-statistics, although it will leave the size of the estimated coefficients unchanged. The intuition is that the same people are in the survey multiple times, which causes a statistical problem as the econometric method assumes we are sampling different people. If we did not do this adjustment this would have the effect of wrongly suggesting statistical significance when it was not present, although practically this has little effect as the standard errors are generally so small.

To adjust for the problem of repeat observations we cluster the standard errors at the level of the household using the *cluster* procedure in the econometric software program STATA. In total there are more than half a million data points for the period 2004–2006.[3] Care has also to be taken because the individual identifiers in the BMCPS are *recycled*, which means that once an individual leaves the survey that number is given to another individual as they join the sample. These individual

---

[3] The data and documentation are downloadable from the NBER website at http://www.nber.org/data/cps_basic.html. The Bureau of Labor Statistics also maintains a CPS website at http://www.bls.census.gov/cps/ with a great deal of information about the survey and access to downloads of recent data.

identifiers are recycled to individuals in the same area. Given this recycling problem we have had to adjust the data a second time to ensure that individuals and households are identified appropriately. We do so by creating a new identifier with the year the household first appears in the data file appended to the end of the original identifier, which solves the problem.

The main results are as follows – where possible we draw direct comparisons with results from the UK, for the same period 2004–2006, in Table A.11.

(1) The self-employment rate of men is higher than it is for women. It rises with age and reaches a maximum of 67.1 in column 1 and 72.5 in column 4. Probabilities are higher for immigrants holding constant characteristics, which was not true in the means.

(2) Self-employment rates for blacks are lower than for whites both in the UK and the US.

(3) In contrast to the UK, self-employment rates are highest for those with professional qualifications such as an MBA and a PhD in the US.

(4) Rates are highest in Montana and California and lowest in West Virginia, Delaware and the District of Columbia.

(5) As in the UK, self-employment rates are highest in Agriculture and Construction and among Artistic and Sporting as well as Sales occupations. They are also high in the US among Personal Care and Service Occupations.

Finally, Table A.15 reports self-employment probabilities across EU member states using data from the Eurobarometer data series. The first column covers data from 14 member countries plus Norway for the period 1974–2002. Column 2 performs a similar exercise, but for a very recent sweep of the Eurobarometer series, from December 2005 to January 2006 and includes a larger sample of countries, including the new East European member states. In both cases the UK is the excluded category. The dependent variable once again is one if self-employed, zero if an employee. The main evidence from this table is as follows:

(1) There has been a declining time trend in the incidence of self-employment across member states.

(2) Self-employment rates are higher for men and for those with less schooling.

(3) There is no evidence that the age squared term is significant – the probability of being self-employed rises linearly with age in each column.

(4) In comparison to the UK, based on column 2, self-employment rates are significantly *higher* in Turkish Cyprus; the Czech Republic; East Germany; Greece; Italy; Poland; Romania and Turkey.

To summarize, self-employment probabilities in the UK rise with age, are high for men, whites, immigrants, individuals with trade apprenticeships, workers in the South West and London as well as in Agriculture and Construction. Occupations with high self-employment rates include Health Professionals; Construction Trades; Hairdressers; Artistic and Sports Occupations and Agricultural Occupations. Broadly similar patterns are found in both the US and the EU.

6

Liquidity Constraints

Even though approximately one worker in eight is self-employed in the UK there appears to remain a strong desire among employees to be self-employed. Blanchflower et al. (2001) examined data from the 1997/1998 International Social Survey Programme and found that nearly half of employees in the UK expressed a desire to be self-employed. New data have recently become available from five sweeps of the Entrepreneurship Flash Eurobarometers on the same issue. There is consistent evidence in Table A.16 from both data sources that approximately half of all wage workers in the UK say they would prefer to be self-employed; this pattern is repeated in other countries in the survey and is especially high in the US and Portugal.[1]

This raises an important puzzle. Why do so few individuals manage to translate their preferences into action? Lack of start-up capital appears to be one likely explanation.

In work based on US micro-data at the level of the individual, Evans and Jovanovic (1989), and Evans and Leighton (1989), have argued that entrepreneurs face liquidity constraints. The authors use

---

[1] Sample sizes in Table A.16 are as follows: column 2, $n = 32,606$; column 3, $n = 31,868$; column 4, $n = 31,604$.

the National Longitudinal Survey of Young Men for 1966–1981, and the Current Population Surveys for 1968–1987. The key test shows that, all else remaining equal, people with greater family assets are more likely to switch to self-employment from employment. This asset variable enters probit equations significantly and with a quadratic form. Although Evans and his collaborators draw the conclusion that capital and liquidity constraints bind, this claim is open to the objection that other interpretations of their correlation are feasible. One possibility, for example, is that inherently acquisitive individuals both start their own businesses and forego leisure to build up family assets. In this case, there would be a correlation between family assets and movement into self-employment even if capital constraints did not exist. A second possibility is that the correlation between family assets and the movement to self-employment arises because children tend to inherit family firms. Parker (2002) provides some much needed theory on whether banks ration enterprises.

Blanchflower and Oswald (1998), find that the probability of self-employment depends positively upon whether the individual ever received an inheritance or gift. Burke et al. (2000; 2002) replicate the findings using the same data source. Work by Holtz-Eakin et al. (1994a, 1994b), drew similar conclusions using different methods on US data. Lindh and Ohlsson (1996) adopt the Blanchflower–Oswald procedure and provide complementary evidence for Sweden. Bernhardt (1994), in a study for Canada, using data from the 1981 Social Change in Canada Project also found evidence that capital constraints appear to bind. And Kidd (1993) also reported that the availability of capital in Australia is a significant barrier to self-employment.

Taylor (2001), in an interesting paper that uses the British Household Panel Study for the period 1994–1996, explores the impact of windfall gains on self-employment. A windfall payment is defined as being from a personal accident claim; a redundancy payment; an annual/seasonal bonus from employment; a win on the football pools; national lottery or other sort of gambling; or anything else. Taylor finds that the size of the payment received has a positive, and concave, impact on the probability of entering self-employment and on the performance of an existing self-employed enterprise, once again consistent with the liquidity constraint hypothesis. Georgellis et al. (2005) extend Taylor's analysis to the later period 1994–2000. The authors find evidence of significant capital constraints – windfalls raise the probability of transition into self-employment at a decreasing rate.

Johansson (2000a, 2000b), in studies for Finland, used a unique data file drawn from the Longitudinal Employment Statistics, compiled by Statistics Finland. It covers the years 1987–1995 and includes, in principle, every individual who has had a job in Finland during the period – it is the *population*. A sample of just over 100,000 workers aged 18–65 was randomly selected and they were followed from 1987 to 1994. Johannsson's empirical strategy was to model the probability of an individual entering self-employment. The main result from the study was that a higher level of wealth significantly increased the probability that an individual made a transition from wage-employment to self-employment. Yannis and Wall (2005) find that capital constraints in Germany based on the GSOEP are especially important for men in explaining movements into self-employment. Moreover Holtz-Eakin and Rosen (2005), also using the GSOEP, found that German workers faced capital constraints that are more severe than those faced by American workers.

Hurst and Lusardi (2004) have claimed that there is little evidence that lack of wealth constrains entrepreneurship apart from at the top of the wealth distribution – above the 95th percentile. They make this claim using data from the Panel Study of Income Dynamics for the period 1989–1994, which contains only 7,500 observations. Very few people in their data – only 304 or 4% – actually transit into self-employment. It appears that their results are driven entirely by measurement error and hence should be ignored. Not finding evidence for something in a poorly specified equation tells us little or nothing about the role of capital constraints or of wealth in setting up a business. Indeed, Fairlie and Krashinsky (2006) examined this issue in some detail. They demonstrate that, using the PSID also, and bifurcating the sample into workers who enter self-employment after job loss and those who do not reveals steadily increasing entry rates as assets increase in both sub-samples. They argue that these two groups merit a separate analysis, because the two groups face different incentives, and thus have different solutions to the entrepreneurial decision. Second, they used micro-data from matched Current Population Surveys (1993–2004) to demonstrate that housing appreciation measured at the MSA-level is a significantly *positive* determinant of entry into self-employment. Their estimates indicate that a 10% annual increase in housing equity increases the mean probability of entrepreneurship by roughly 20% and that the effect is not concentrated at the upper tail of the distribution. Fairlie and Krashinsky's (2006) findings on the relationship between housing appreciation and entrepreneurship are consistent with the liquidity constraint hypothesis.

Using the 1991 French Household Survey of Financial Assets, Laferrere and McEntee (1995), examined the determinants of self-employment using data on intergenerational transfers of wealth, education, informal human capital and a range of demographic variables. They also find evidence of the importance played by the family in the decision to enter self-employment. Intergenerational transfers of wealth, familial transfers of human capital, and the structure of the family were found to be the determining factors in the decision to move from wage work into entrepreneurship.

Broussard et al. (2003) found that the self-employed in the US have between 0.2 and 0.4 more children compared to the non-self-employed. The authors argue that having more children can increase the likelihood that an inside family member will be a good match at running the business. One might also think that the existence of family businesses, which are particularly prevalent in farming, is a further way to overcome the existence of capital constraints. Transfers of firms within families will help to preserve the status quo and will work against the interests of blacks in particular, who do not have as strong a history of business ownership as indigenous whites.

Analogously, Hout and Rosen (2000) found that the offspring of self-employed fathers are more likely than others to become self-employed (see also Dunn and Holtz-Eakin, 2000). These studies generally find that an individual who had a self-employed parent is roughly two to three times more likely to be self-employed than someone who did not have a self-employed parent. More recently Fairlie and Robb (2006) have demonstrated, using data from the 1992 Characteristics of Business Owners (CBO) Survey, that more than half of all business owners had a self-employed family member prior to starting their business. Conditional on having a self-employed family member, less than 50% of small business owners worked in that family member's business suggesting that it is unlikely that intergenerational links in self-employment are largely the result of the acquisition of general and specific business human capital and that instead similarities across family members in entrepreneurial preferences may explain part of the relationship. In contrast, estimates from regression models *conditioning* on business ownership indicated that having a self-employed family member plays only a minor role in determining small business outcomes, whereas the human capital acquired from prior work experience in a family member's business appears to be very important for business success. Estimates from the CBO also indicated that only 1.6% of all small businesses are inherited suggesting that the role of business inheritances in determining intergenerational links in self-employment is limited at best.

Fairlie and Meyer (2000), rule out a number of explanations for the difference in the self-employment rates of white and black males. They found that trends in demographic factors, including the Great Migration and the racial convergence in education levels "did not have large effects on the trend in the racial gap in self-employment" (p. 662). They also found that an initial lack of business experience "cannot explain the current low levels of black self-employment." Further they found that "the lack of traditions in business enterprise among blacks that resulted from slavery cannot explain a substantial part of the current racial gap in self-employment" (p. 664). Fairlie (1999) and Wainwright (2000) have shown that a considerable part of the explanation of the differences between the African American and white self-employment rate can be attributed to discrimination. Bates (1989) finds strong supporting evidence that racial differences in levels of financial capital have significant effects upon racial patterns in business failure rates. Fairlie (1999) also found that the black exit rate from self-employment is twice as high as that of whites.

Using the same 1992 Characteristics of Business Owners (CBO) Survey, Fairlie and Robb (2005) examined why African–American owned businesses lag substantially behind white-owned businesses in sales, profits, employment, and survival. Black business owners, they found, were much less likely than white owners to have had a self-employed family member prior to starting their business and are less likely to have worked in that family member's business. They found further that the lack of prior work experience in a family business among black business owners, perhaps by limiting their acquisition of general and specific business human capital, negatively affects black business outcomes.

Blanchflower et al. (2003) examined the availability of credit to minority and female-owned small businesses using data from the 1993 to 1998 National Surveys of Small Business Finances conducted by the Reserve Board of Governors. They demonstrated that loan denial probabilities for African–American owned firms are approximately double those for comparable white-owned firms. Even when African–Americans were able to obtain loans they have to pay higher interest rates. Comparable, but smaller effects are found for Hispanics. These differences were not explained by differences in creditworthiness or other observables. Such differences disappeared when the use of credit cards was examined, where the banks were unaware of the race of the applicant. The authors found that firms owned by minorities are discriminated against in the credit market. Similar results were found by Cavalluzzo et al. (2002).

A recent study published by the US Chamber of Commerce (2005) confirms the findings in Blanchflower et al. (2003). The survey was conducted in March and April 2005 and detailed the financing problems experienced by small business owners, 95% of whom had less than 100 employees: 1,080 business owners were interviewed and reported that minority businesses rely heavily on credit cards to fund their businesses, often do not apply for credit, even though they need it, for fear of being denied and were especially likely to need working capital. In particular they report that the availability of credit is their top problem, exactly as reported by Blanchflower et al. (2003). The biggest difference in responses between minorities and Caucasian men and women was availability of credit: 19% of Caucasian males report credit as their top problem compared with 54% for minority males – a 35 percentage point difference. There was a 15 percentage point difference for women. In no other category is there more than a 10 percentage point difference for men or women.

It is appropriate to examine some new empirical evidence which appears to support the proposition that liquidity constraints bind on small businesses. First, we examine the impact of inheritances and gifts and then the role of rising house prices and find they both appear to generate more self-employment.

Table A.17 uses new evidence from the National Child Development Study (NCDS) on the incidence of self-employment among workers in their mid forties. The NCDS is a birth cohort study covering every individual born in the week 3rd–9th March 1958. Blanchflower and Oswald (1998) examined the impact of inheritances and gifts on the probability of an individual being self-employed on sweeps four and five conducted at ages 23 and 33, respectively. In that paper it was found that an exogenous shock or windfall in the form of an inheritance or gift – received at any point from birth to age 23 – and expressed in 1981 pounds raised the probability of self-employment. New data have recently become available on the seventh sweep of the NCDS conducted in 2004/2005 when the respondents were aged 46 or 47. It turns out that the higher the value of an inheritance or gift the higher is the probability of self-employment not only at ages 23 and 33 but also, more than 20 years later, at age 46/47. This result remains even when controlling for education and the social class of the respondent's mother's husband (usually the father) when the respondent was aged 11. Having a father who was self-employed – even when the respondent was young, at age 11 – raises the probability of the respondent being self-employed 35 years later. It turns out, also that a Copying Design test score conducted at age 11 is a significant predictor of whether or not the respondent is self-employed 35 years later. Other controls including Verbal and Non-Verbal IQ, Math and Reading test scores at ages 7, 11, and 16 were everywhere insignificant. Results are the same in column 4 when the dependent variable is set to zero not only for employees, but also for the unemployed and those who are OLF. Lack of start-up capital is a likely explanation why individual's ambitions to be self-employed do not meet fruition. Blanchflower and Oswald (1998) also found that when directly questioned in interview surveys, potential entrepreneurs say that raising capital is their principal problem.

Another type of windfall is an increase in house prices, which may help home owners to overcome capital constraints by releasing home equity. Rising house prices, for example, enable liquidity constrained nascent entrepreneurs to start a business, or even to enable it to survive. Black et al. (1996), for example, found that a 10% rise in the value of housing equity increased the number of new firm VAT registrations in the UK by some 5%. Taylor (2004) found that an increase in house prices increased the probability of self-employment entry. Chart A.8 above suggested that, at the national level, changes in self-employment and nominal house price inflation moved reasonably closely together. The self-employment rate ticked up in 2005 as house prices rose and fell at the end of the 1980s as house prices fell.

We explore this relationship more closely in Table A.18, where we regress the log of the self-employment rate, defined by region and year, on the (log) house price and the log of the regional unemployment rate, as well as a full set of year dummies and a lagged dependent variable. The year dummies can be thought of as proxying inflation, so the house price variable should be thought of as being in real terms. The year dummies will also capture any time-variant, year-specific factors that affect all regions symmetrically – such as changes in legislation.

In each of the columns 1–4, the house price variable enters significantly, with or without a lagged dependent variable or with region fixed effects. The unemployment rate is significant in columns 1 and 3 (although of opposite sign), but not in the presence of the lagged dependent variable. The unemployment rate does become significant in column 5, however, where the year dummies are replaced with an (insignificant) price deflator, but this equation fails to account for the effects of legislative changes. The house price elasticity of our preferred equation (column 4) means that a doubling of house prices leads to an increase in the self-employment rate of 9.5%, so the effect isn't small. We take this as evidence of liquidity constraints being eased for nascent entrepreneurs as house prices rise, entirely consistent with the findings of Black et al. (1996) for the period 1966–1990, Cowling and Mitchell (1997) for the period 1972–1992, and Taylor (2004) for the period 1970–2001. Henley (2005) also shows the importance of housing wealth for the self-employed in job creation. It is also consistent with Fairlie and Krashinsky's (2006) findings for the US on the positive relationship between housing appreciation and the prevalence of entrepreneurship.

Between 2005Q1 and 2007Q1 approximately 70% of the growth in total UK employment has been from self-employment (217k out of 305k), raising the self-employment rate from 12.6 percentage points to 13.2 percentage points, which is an increase of 4.9%. Over the same period aggregate UK house prices have appreciated by 14.7%. Solving out the long run elasticity of the self-employment rate wrt to (log) house prices from column 4 of Table A.18, gives $+0.171$[2]:

$$\text{In self-employment rate}_t = 0.4440 \text{ ln self-employment rate}_{t-1}$$
$$+\, 0.0952 \text{ ln house prices}_t.$$

To give an indication of how to interpret the size of this elasticity of 0.171, such a number means that if house prices double the associated long-run impact is to increase the self-employment rate by approximately a sixth. This elasticity therefore suggests that rising house prices can potentially explain approximately half ($14.7 * 0.171 = 2.5\%$) of the observed 4.9% increase in the UK self-employment rate between 2005 and 2007. Liquidity constraints continue to bind for small-businesses in the UK.

---

[2] $0.0952/(1 - 0.4440)$

7

Discussion and Conclusions

Self-employment rose sharply in the UK during the 1980s, encouraged by focused government intervention and supported by financial liberalization. The period was also characterized by sustained and rapid economic growth. But did greater self-employment cause heightened growth?

Greater numbers of self-employed workers in an economy should, in theory, increase labor market flexibility in response to demand shocks because there is no binding wage contract on the number of hours worked. In turn, Millard (2000) argues that this should lead to greater output and consumption and lower unemployment. There is no empirical evidence to support such a theoretical proposition. As we noted above, self-employment appears to be uncorrelated with unemployment, although transitions between employees and self-employment are negatively correlated with unemployment, while transitions from unemployment to self-employment are positively correlated. In aggregate these two effects roughly cancel each other out. What about any relationship with output?

Evidence from a series of GDP growth equations for 23 countries over the period 1966–1996 presented in Blanchflower (2000) suggested that a higher self-employment rate does not increase the real growth rate of the economy; in fact there was even some evidence to the contrary.[1] We repeat this analysis here for a longer time period and more countries. Table A.19 examines the relationship between the growth in real GDP and changes in the self-employment rate, using time series data on the 30 OECD countries for the period 1967–2005 (the additional seven countries are Czech Republic, Hungary, Korea, Mexico, Poland, Slovakia, and Switzerland). As in Blanchflower (2000), the regressions should be thought of as a Cobb–Douglas production function, where the change in the numbers of employees over the previous period is included to distinguish the labor input. Capital is assumed to grow linearly and as the model is estimated in changes the effect of capital will be in the constant. Also included in the regressions are a set of country dummies plus a lagged dependent variable. The columns in Table A.19 experiment with different measures of self-employment. Columns 1 and 2 define self-employment as the number of self-employed as a percentage of total employment. Columns 3 and 4 define self-employment as the number of *non-agricultural* self-employed as a percentage of total *non-agricultural* employment.[2] These results presume a particular direction of causation, from self-employment to growth and not the reverse. Columns 1 and 3 include the change in the self-employment rate and a lagged GDP term. Columns 2 and 4 add the change in the number of employees. In no case is the change in the self-employment rate significant: experimenting with longer lags produced similar results. The results confirm Blanchflower's (2000) earlier findings, but for a richer data set – we find *no evidence* that changes in self-employment are correlated with changes in real GDP.

Another measure of economic benefit could be greater happiness. Table A.20 presents evidence on life satisfaction using data from the Eurobarometer trend file of 1970–2002 for 16 European countries in column 1 and for the UK in column 2. The final column uses data from the most recently available (14th) sweep of the British House-

---

[1] The 23 countries were Australia, Austria, Belgium, Canada, Denmark, Eire, Finland, France, Germany, Greece, Iceland, Italy, Japan, Luxembourg, Netherlands, New Zealand, Norway, Portugal, Spain, Sweden, Turkey, UK, and the USA.

[2] A split excluding non-agricultural data is not available for Switzerland.

hold Panel Study of 2004/2005. In all three columns the self-employed have significantly higher life satisfaction than do employees. So can a higher self-employment rate lead to greater aggregate happiness? The results are not supportive. We substituted mean life satisfaction scores on a four point scale taken from the World Database of Happiness for 1976–2006 for GDP growth and repeated our previous analysis. The question asked was "How satisfied are you with the life you lead?" – very satisfied; fairly satisfied; not very satisfied; not at all satisfied, where very is coded as 4 down through not at all which is coded as 1. We include GDP growth as an explanatory variable, along with inflation and the unemployment rate and a complete set of country and year dummies.[3] Self-employment fails to provide any incremental information in explaining happiness when these other variables are included. We find evidence that both unemployment and inflation lower happiness, although the effect is greater for unemployment than it is for inflation, as found by Di Tella et al. (2001) and Wolfers (2003). The GDP term, which they did not include, enters significantly positive. It remains uncertain why self-employment enters positively into a micro-level happiness equation, but not into a macro-level equation.

These results, of course, do not mean that higher self-employment is a bad thing. A very high proportion of individuals across a number of surveys express the desire to become self-employed. We certainly find no evidence that more self-employment is bad for the economy. The self-employed seem to especially value their independence. Many governments around the world believe that it is appropriate to try

---

[3] The results are as follows, with the dependent variable being the mean life satisfaction score in year t.

Satisfaction$_{t-1}$	0.4501 (8.45)
GDP annual growth rate	0.0060 (2.77)
Inflation rate	−0.0010 (0.66)
Unemployment rate	−0.0053 (2.70)
Self-employment rate	0.0001 (0.03)
Adjusted $R^2 = 0.9623$, $N = 344$	

Includes year and country dummies. Countries are Austria; Belgium; Canada; Denmark; Finland; France; Germany; Greece; Ireland; Italy; Japan; Luxembourg; Netherlands; Portugal; Spain; Sweden; UK and the USA. T-statistics in parentheses.

and make their economies more entrepreneurial, but that need not necessarily imply a higher self-employment rate. And it also means that a higher self-employment rate cannot be expected to translate directly into greater economic success. A lower self-employment rate could conceivably be better. Can we imagine a society consisting almost exclusively of wage and salary workers? It would seem unlikely that a self-employment rate around zero would be optimal. Unfortunately, we have no way of knowing what number governments should be aiming for. Market forces need to prevail and Blanchflower's (2004) conclusion stands; more *may not be* better. Let the market rip.

The probability of being self-employed in the UK is higher for men and rises non-linearly with age. Those with craft qualifications, including trade apprenticeships, are more likely to be self-employed, and rates are higher for those working in the construction or retailing industries. Immigrants are more likely to be self-employed, but there is considerable variation by country of birth. Probabilities are also high in the South West and London as well as in Agriculture and Construction. Occupations with high self-employment rates include Health Professionals; Construction Trades; Hairdressers; Artistic and Sports Occupations and Agricultural Occupations.

In the US, the probabilities are higher the more educated a person is, while the opposite is true in Europe. Financial windfalls or housing capital gains are important explanatory variables for self-employment, through their ability to mitigate liquidity constraints. House price increases appear to be associated with increases in the self-employment rate.

Most self-employed individuals in the UK work alone or in a partnership and do not have any employees. They typically work longer hours than their employed counterparts, but generally earn less. There is, however, no evidence that in aggregate increases in self-employment affect growth in GDP, nor happiness, positively. At the very top end the successful entrepreneur earns considerably more than most wage and salary earners. The entrepreneur has a unique skill – he or she has created a job for him or herself and possibly even a job for others. The entrepreneur is an important engine for growth in the economy.

Appendix

Table A.1 Self-employment as a % of all employment.

Country	1960s	1970s	1980s	1990s	2000s	2005
Australia	14.4	14.1	15.3	14.5	13.1	12.7
Austria	28.3	21.6	13.3	10.5	11.1	11.9
Belgium	17.1	13.6	14.0	14.8	–	–
Canada	13.3	9.5	8.8	10.2	9.6	9.2
Czech Republic	–	–	–	11.7	15.5	15.3
Denmark	18.5	13.7	10.1	8.7	8.0	7.9
Finland	25.8	18.4	13.7	14.2	12.5	12.1
France	24.9	18.7	15.1	11.2	8.9	9.0
Germany	11.1	14.3	10.5	9.5	10.5	11.3
Greece	–	51.9	37.6	34.0	31.1	30.1
Hungary	–	–	–	16.6	13.6	13.4
Iceland	19.1	15.8	13.5	17.0	15.4	14.1
Ireland	30.1	24.8	21.4	20.6	17.0	16.7
Italy	36.4	28.6	24.2	24.6	24.4	25.1
Japan	19.8	18.2	16.0	12.5	10.6	10.2
Korea	35.0	34.1	32.0	27.5	27.5	27.0
Luxembourg	22.2	16.6	11.6	8.3	7.0	6.7*
Mexico	–	18.8	21.7	30.3	29.1	28.5
Netherlands	–	12.5	11.3	10.6	11.1	–
New Zealand	14.1	15.2	17.1	19.6	18.8	17.9
Norway	6.3	12.1	9.7	8.4	7.0	7.2
Poland	34.5	26.6	26.0	24.5	21.9	20.5

58   *Appendix*

Table A.1 (*Continued*).

Country	1960s	1970s	1980s	1990s	2000s	2005
Portugal	25.8	20.8	31.2	25.8	24.4	23.6
Slovakia	–	–	–	6.6	9.8	12.6
Spain	24.3	22.0	22.1	20.7	17.2	16.6
Sweden	10.8	7.6	7.7	10.0	9.6	9.6
Switzerland	–	–	–	9.9	10.0	9.3
Turkey	–	–	29.8	29.9	29.7	29.8
UK	7.1	8.0	10.8	13.3	12.3	12.8
USA	10.6	8.6	8.7	8.3	7.3	7.4

Source: OECD Labour Force Statistics.
*Luxembourg, 2004.

Table A.2 Self-employment as a % of all non-agricultural employment.

Country	1960s	1970s	1980s	1990s	2000s	2005
Australia	10.0	10.5	12.2	12.2	11.5	11.4
Austria	13.3	10.6	7.3	6.8	8.1	8.8
Belgium	14.0	11.3	12.3	13.6	–	–
Canada	7.7	6.3	6.9	8.7	8.7	8.4
Czech Republic	–	–	–	11.7	15.4	15.2
Denmark	12.4	9.5	7.3	6.9	6.9	6.9
Finland	–	6.3	7.1	9.9	9.5	9.6
France	14.0	11.3	9.9	8.2	7.0	7.1
Germany	8.6	9.0	8.1	8.6	9.9	10.7
Greece	–	31.6	27.9	27.4	25.0	24.8
Hungary	–	–	–	15.3	12.3	12.4
Iceland	9.7	8.8	8.8	14.2	13.1	11.9
Ireland	10.3	10.2	11.3	13.3	12.8	12.9
Italy	25.7	21.9	21.0	22.8	23.3	24.2
Japan	14.5	13.9	13.0	10.2	8.8	8.5
Korea	–	–	25.5	23.1	24.2	23.9
Luxembourg	13.4	10.7	8.3	6.8	6.0	5.8*
Mexico	–	16.6	14.3	25.1	25.8	25.3
Netherlands	–	8.9	8.5	9.0	9.9	–
New Zealand	8.3	8.8	11.9	15.8	16.0	15.6
Norway	–	7.4	6.5	5.8	5.1	5.6
Poland	2.8	2.6	4.8	11.2	11.8	11.3
Portugal	14.9	12.4	16.3	18.3	17.2	16.4
Slovakia	–	–	–	6.6	9.8	12.6
Spain	–	15.7	17.2	17.8	15.4	15.2
Sweden	7.1	4.7	5.3	8.5	8.6	8.8
Turkey	–	–	26.0	25.2	22.9	23.2
UK	5.9	7.0	9.9	12.5	11.8	12.2
USA	8.1	6.9	7.5	7.3	6.7	6.8

Source: OECD Labour Force Statistics.
*Luxembourg, 2004.

Table A.3 Self-employment # (000s) and as a % of all UK employment.

1962	1,854 (7.43%)
1963	1,840 (7.36%)
1964	1,827 (7.21%)
1965	1,813 (7.04%)
1966	1,818 (7.10%)
1967	1,875 (7.43%)
1968	1,917 (7.64%)
1969	2,018 (8.05%)
1970	2,044 (8.20%)
1971	2,004 (8.18%)
1972	2,080 (8.46%)
1973	2,114 (8.47%)
1974	2,091 (8.35%)
1975	2,057 (8.25%)
1976	2,055 (8.29%)
1977	2,055 (8.28%)
1978	2,034 (8.15%)
1979	2,084 (8.27%)
1980	2,205 (8.79%)
1981	2,316 (9.48%)
1982	2,387 (9.97%)
1983	2,478 (10.42%)
1984	2,744 (11.30%)
1985	2,844 (11.56%)
1986	2,909 (11.75%)
1987	3,151 (12.48%)
1988	3,297 (12.64%)
1989	3,532 (13.20%)
1990	3,761 (14.00%)
1991	3,669 (14.02%)
1992	3,461 (13.55%)
1993	3,403 (13.45%)
1994	3,514 (13.78%)
1995	3,551 (13.76%)
1996	3,510 (13.47%)
1997	3,458 (13.04%)
1998	3,352 (12.51%)
1999	3,311 (12.19%)
2000	3,260 (11.87%)
2001	3,300 (11.91%)
2002	3,344 (11.98%)
2003	3,573 (12.68%)
2004	3,630 (12.75%)
2005	3,653 (12.71%)
2006	3,753 (12.96%)

Source: Labor Force Survey and various editions of the Employment Gazette.
Notes: These annual numbers are averages of quarterly data.

Table A.4 Survival rates of VAT registered enterprises up to 10 years, whole of UK.

| | Percent still trading | | | | | | | | | | |
| | Year of registration | | | | | | | | | | |
	1995	1996	1997	1998	1999	2000	2001	2002	2003	2004	2005
6 months	94.7	94.9	95.5	95.7	95.8	96.0	96.5	97.2	97.8	97.9	98.6
12 months	88.1	88.3	89.7	89.9	90.1	90.5	91.4	92.1	93.0	92.1	
18 months	81.2	82.1	83.8	83.9	84.1	84.8	85.9	86.6	87.0	86.9	
24 months	75.2	76.5	78.1	78.1	78.4	79.1	80.0	81.1	81.9		
30 months	69.9	71.3	73.1	72.6	73.0	73.6	74.5	76.0	77.5		
36 months	65.6	66.9	68.5	67.7	68.3	68.4	69.7	71.3			
42 months	61.7	62.8	64.2	63.2	63.6	63.8	65.1	67.7			
48 months	58.3	59.2	60.3	59.2	59.5	59.8	61.2				
54 months	55.1	55.8	56.8	55.4	55.7	56.1	58.2				
60 months	52.2	52.6	53.3	51.9	52.4	53.0					
66 months	49.5	49.9	50.2	48.9	49.5	50.7					
72 months	47.0	47.2	47.3	46.2	47.0						
78 months	44.7	44.7	44.7	43.7	45.1						
84 months	42.5	42.4	42.5	41.6							
90 months	40.3	40.3	40.3	39.9							
96 months	38.4	38.4	38.5								
102 months	36.5	36.7	37.1								
108 months	34.9	35.1									
114 months	33.4	33.9									
120 months	32.1										

Source: DTI Small Business Service, February 2007; http://www.dtistats.net/smes/200702/

Table A.5 Loan Guarantee Scheme loans since 1995–1996.

	Number of guaranteed loans	Value (£ million)	Number of loans to start-ups	Value to start ups (£ million)	Number of loans defaulted/claims made
1995–1996	7,484	na	na	na	814
1996–1997	6,942	na	na	na	1,642
1997–1998	5,081	201.34	1,378	39.09	2,085
1998–1999	4,482	188.80	1,209	37.62	1,957
1999–2000	4,279	205.99	1,180	40.34	1,779
2000–2001	4,312	240.46	1,323	53.17	1,531
2001–2002	4,369	254.69	1,286	53.857	1,624
2002–2003	3,616	269.461	1,024	50.719	1,690
2003–2004	5,966	409.258	1,850	42.205	1,578

Source: House of Commons Publications.

Table A.6 Self-employment in the UK as a % of total employment by industry.

		1985	1990	1995	2000	2005
A,B	Agriculture, fishing etc.	47.5	54.5	54.0	46.7	52.1
C,E	Mining, quarrying, and utilities	1.0	3.5	2.6	2.7	3.2
D	Manufacturing	4.3	6.2	5.5	5.2	6.0
F	Construction	31.0	40.7	45.7	33.3	37.1
G,H	Wholesale, retail & hotels and rest.	17.2	15.9	14.8	11.9	10.7
I	Transport, storage & communications	7.7	11.4	12.7	11.5	12.5
J,K	Financial int. & business services	12.3	14.9	15.5	14.8	16.5
L–N	Public sector	3.7	na	5.0	4.8	4.5
O,Q	Other	21.4	na	24.9	24.7	26.2
	All industries	11.6	14.0	13.8	11.9	12.7

Source: Labour Force Survey.

Table A.7 Proportion of total UK self-employment by industry (%).

	1995	1996	1997	1998	1999	2000	2001	2002	2003	2004	2005	2006
Agriculture, hunting & forestry	7.3	7.0	6.8	6.4	5.6	5.4	5.2	5.0	5.0	5.0	5.2	5.1
Fishing	0.3	0.3	0.3	0.3	0.3	0.3	0.2	0.3	0.3	0.2	0.2	0.2
Mining & quarrying	0.2	0.1	0.2	0.1	0.1	0.1	0.2	0.2	0.1	0.1	0.2	0.2
Manufacturing	7.6	7.6	7.8	8.6	7.9	7.3	6.8	7.0	6.7	6.7	6.3	6.9
Electricity gas & water supply	0.1	0.1	0.1	0.2	0.1	0.1	0.2	0.2	0.1	0.1	0.1	0.1
Construction	23.0	23.3	21.3	19.9	19.8	19.7	20.6	21.8	22.0	23.1	23.3	23.0
Wholesale, retail & motor trade	16.0	14.6	15.2	15.3	15.2	15.2	14.6	13.9	13.2	13.0	12.4	11.7
Hotels & restaurants	4.9	4.9	5.1	4.3	3.8	3.6	3.6	3.4	3.6	3.6	3.3	2.9
Transport, storage & communication	5.9	5.9	6.4	6.3	6.5	6.7	7.0	7.2	7.0	6.7	6.8	7.7
Financial intermediation	1.3	1.1	1.3	1.4	1.2	1.4	1.6	1.3	1.4	1.5	1.5	1.2
Real estate, renting & business activities	14.1	14.8	15.4	16.6	17.6	17.7	17.7	17.9	18.6	18.2	18.8	19.1
Public administration & defence	0.4	0.5	0.3	0.4	0.5	0.5	0.5	0.5	0.6	0.6	0.6	0.7
Education	2.2	2.4	2.5	2.6	3.0	2.8	2.4	2.5	3.0	2.9	2.7	3.2
Health & social work	6.3	6.5	6.7	6.7	6.6	7.0	7.1	6.5	6.3	6.4	6.7	5.9
Other community, social & personal	8.7	8.8	8.8	9.1	9.9	10.3	10.4	10.5	10.1	9.8	10.2	10.2
Private households with employed persons	1.7	1.9	1.8	1.8	1.8	1.8	1.8	1.8	1.9	2.0	1.8	1.8
Extra-territorial organizations, bodies	0.0	0.0	0.0	0.0	0.0	0.0	0.0	0.0	0.0	0.0	0.0	0.0
Workplace outside UK	0.1	0.1	0.0	0.0	0.1	0.1	0.0	0.0	0.1	0.0	0.0	0.0

Source: Labour Force Survey.

Table A.8 The % of self-employed workers who had been employees a year earlier.

1986	7.6%	1997	7.0%
1987	7.9%	1998	7.8%
1988	8.9%	1999	8.0%
1989	9.4%	2000	8.5%
1990	9.6%	2001	8.8%
1991	7.6%	2002	9.3%
1992	8.6%	2003	9.2%
1993	7.5%	2004	8.5%
1994	6.8%	2005	8.7%
1995	7.7%	2006	8.2%
1996	7.5%		

Source: Labour Force Survey microdata Spring quarters – own calculations (weighted).

Table A.9 UK and US weighted self-employment rates by country of birth (ages 16–70), 2004–2006.

	UK	US
Total	12.7%	10.6%
Non-immigrant	12.5%	10.6%
Immigrants	14.5%	10.1%
UK		12.8%
USA	17.6%	
Argentina	12.6%	7.3%
Armenia	9.2%	22.2%
Australia	14.6%	9.2%
Austria	19.5%	14.3%
Bangladesh	17.6%	11.0%
Barbados	3.7%	21.9%
Belgium	8.0%	20.8%
Brazil	8.5%	9.6%
Burma/Myanmar	12.5%	13.0%
Canada	16.9%	5.2%
Caribbean Commonwealth	4.6%	18.5%
Chile	5.0%	11.4%
China	12.8%	14.2%
Columbia	11.5%	18.8%
Cuba	17.0%	10.8%
Denmark	21.0%	10.2%
Egypt	26.2%	15.8%
Ethiopia	14.8%	12.2%
Finland	1.4%	12.7%
Former Czechoslovakia	5.2%	9.9%
Former USSR etc.	23.0%	15.1%
France	10.4%	10.8%
Germany	12.5%	9.4%
Ghana	7.8%	10.3%
Greece	18.0%	11.9%

Table A.9 (*Continued*).

	UK	US
Guyana	15.2%	26.2%
Hong Kong	16.8%	26.6%
Hungary	15.0%	4.3%
India	13.3%	25.1%
Indonesia	14.7%	16.1%
Iran	31.7%	21.3%
Iraq	22.6%	5.3%
Irish Republic	18.4%	7.9%
Israel	21.0%	13.4%
Italy	19.8%	28.1%
Jamaica	12.6%	17.6%
Japan	8.3%	10.2%
Kenya	18.1%	12.8%
Korea	17.5%	12.5%
Latvia	13.2%	14.3%
Lebanon	21.5%	26.4%
Lithuania	24.9%	4.6%
Malaysia	11.3%	14.0%
Mexico	14.0%	3.0%
Morocco	13.4%	8.3%
Netherlands	13.1%	6.8%
New Zealand	16.5%	6.8%
Nigeria	8.9%	7.1%
Norway	19.8%	10.3%
Pakistan	30.7%	5.5%
Philippines	3.4%	8.0%
Poland	16.1%	10.1%
Portugal	7.4%	5.9%
Romania	43.9%	7.4%
Singapore	11.1%	7.6%
Slovakia	2.6%	7.0%
South Africa	11.3%	10.6%
Spain	9.6%	9.1%
Sweden	10.8%	29.7%
Switzerland	19.6%	3.9%
Thailand	31.5%	13.9%
Trinidad & Tobago	10.7%	12.0%
Turkey	26.5%	22.1%
Ukraine	14.8%	9.9%
Venezuela	22.8%	11.7%
Vietnam	14.4%	27.8%
Correlation $= -0.0044$		

Source: UK Labour Force Surveys, 2004–2006 and US Basic Monthly files of the Current Population Survey, 2004–2006.

Table A.10 Self-employment dprobits, 1994-1996.

	(1)	(2)	(3)	(4)
Age	0.0102 (51.34)	0.0101 (50.89)	0.0123 (67.28)	0.0084 (54.18)
Age^2	−0.00008 (32.54)	−0.00009 (32.20)	−0.0001 (47.39)	−0.00006 (35.90)
Male	0.0933 (119.37)	0.0935 (119.66)	0.0568 (74.14)	0.0169 (22.52)
Asian	0.0654 (22.69)	0.0349 (11.36)	0.0657 (21.55)	0.0406 (16.05)
Black	−0.0461 (13.27)	−0.0583 (17.22)	−0.0436 (13.89)	−0.0288 (11.21)
Chinese	0.1637 (17.87)	0.1206 (13.62)	0.1102 (13.65)	0.1282 (16.59)
Other race	0.0047 (1.07)	−0.0165 (3.87)	−0.0104 (2.68)	−0.0098 (3.15)
1995	−0.0014 (1.58)	−0.0013 (1.47)	−0.0015 (1.87)	−0.0007 (1.08)
1996	−0.0041 (4.65)	−0.0040 (4.53)	−0.0037 (4.52)	−0.0022 (3.32)
Immigrant		0.0337 (18.51)	0.0263 (15.82)	0.0174 (12.75)
Higher education	−0.0311 (20.80)	−0.0306 (20.41)	−0.0280 (20.54)	−0.0102 (8.45)
GCSE A level or equiv.	0.0336 (26.93)	0.0346 (27.68)	−0.0040 (3.64)	0.0072 (6.63)
GCSE grades A-C or equiv.	−0.0093 (7.02)	−0.0080 (6.02)	−0.0316 (27.25)	0.0019 (1.66)
Other qualifications	−0.0170 (12.70)	−0.0180 (13.40)	−0.0401 (34.45)	−0.0089 (7.58)
No qualification	−0.0010 (0.82)	−0.0003 (0.27)	−0.0358 (30.86)	−0.0038 (3.13)
Do not know	0.0033 (0.34)	0.0046 (0.47)	−0.0311 (4.01)	−0.0085 (1.20)
Regions				
Rest of North			0.0409 (10.35)	0.0312 (9.35)
South Yorkshire			0.0415 (9.56)	0.0384 (10.21)
West Yorkshire			0.0391 (10.06)	0.0344 (10.34)
Rest Yorks & Humber			0.0471 (11.46)	0.0371 (10.59)
East Midlands			0.0446 (12.31)	0.0396 (12.73)
East Anglia			0.0625 (15.64)	0.0557 (15.96)
Inner London			0.0804 (18.95)	0.0538 (15.21)
Outer London			0.0577 (15.50)	0.0537 (16.51)
Rest of South East			0.0632 (18.52)	0.0590 (19.94)
South West			0.0920 (23.66)	0.0796 (23.28)

Table A.10 (*Continued*).

	(1)	(2)	(3)	(4)
West Midlands			0.0313 (8.28)	0.0302 (9.31)
Rest West Midlands			0.0636 (16.25)	0.0590 (17.14)
Greater Manchester			0.0415 (10.81)	0.0363 (11.03)
Merseyside			0.0330 (7.70)	0.0312 (8.46)
Rest of North West			0.0508 (13.08)	0.0406 (12.25)
Wales			0.0713 (17.73)	0.0558 (16.16)
Strathclyde			0.0129 (3.50)	0.0172 (5.42)
Rest of Scotland			0.0167 (4.82)	0.0178 (6.04)
Northern Ireland			0.0728 (13.93)	0.0697 (14.95)
Industries				
Energy & water			−0.1016 (72.52)	−0.0662 (39.86)
Manufacturing			−0.1635 (141.31)	−0.0860 (47.13)
Construction			−0.0381 (20.89)	0.0037 (1.25)
Distribution			−0.1210 (88.27)	−0.0515 (22.76)
Transport			−0.1051 (95.89)	−0.0465 (21.80)
Banking			−0.1127 (89.87)	−0.0316 (13.11)
Public administration			−0.1851 (138.14)	−0.1032 (51.38)
Other services			−0.0780 (53.07)	−0.0328 (14.22)
Occupations				
Workplace outside UK			−0.0865 (12.89)	−0.0278 (3.24)
Prod managers – manufacturing etc.				0.0121 (3.30)
Specialist managers				0.0106 (3.22)
Financial & office managers etc.				−0.0356 (12.15)
Managers in transport and storing				−0.0277 (6.99)
Managers in farming, horticulture etc.				0.6248 (57.03)
Managers etc. service industry				0.3574 (57.96)
Managers, administrators nes				0.0621 (12.71)
Natural scientists				0.0064 (1.20)
Engineers and technologists				0.0653 (15.22)

Table A.10 (*Continued*).

	(1)	(2)	(3)	(4)
Librarians etc. professionals				−0.0493 (5.78)
Professional occupations nes				0.0339 (6.43)
Scientific technicians				−0.0254 (6.25)
Draughtspersons, surveyors etc.				0.0522 (8.81)
Computer analysts, programmers				0.0004 (0.11)
Ship, aircraft officers & controllers				0.0000 (0.01)
Health associate professionals				0.1023 (20.27)
Legal associate professionals				−0.0211 (2.74)
Business, finance associate profs				0.0413 (9.43)
Welfare etc. associate professionals				0.2585 (34.28)
Artistic, sports etc. professionals				0.4088 (57.52)
Prof, technical occupations nes				0.1980 (31.17)
Administrative staff in government				−0.0633 (13.58)
Numerical clerks and cashiers				−0.0142 (4.77)
Filing and record clerks				−0.0400 (11.30)
Clerks nes				−0.0307 (9.90)
Stores, despatch clerks & keepers				−0.0607 (18.81)
Secretarial etc. personnel				−0.0200 (6.53)
Receptionist, telephonists etc.				−0.0506 (14.13)
Clerical, secretarial occupations nes				−0.0483 (10.21)
Construction trades				0.4576 (62.54)
Metal machining, fitting etc. trades				0.0551 (12.70)
Electrical, electronic trades				0.0867 (18.82)
Metal forming, welding etc. trades				0.1824 (31.12)
Vehicle trades				0.1407 (24.56)
Textiles, garments etc. trades				0.1800 (28.00)
Printing and related trades				0.0813 (12.20)

Table A.10 (*Continued*).

	(1)	(2)	(3)	(4)
Woodworking trades				0.3871 (52.08)
Food preparation trades				0.1013 (13.37)
Other craft, related trades nes				0.1744 (29.46)
Health professionals				0.5341 (62.93)
Teaching professionals				0.0777 (17.62)
Legal professionals				0.2947 (35.42)
Business & financial professionals				0.1457 (26.12)
Architects, town planners, surveyors				0.1190 (18.63)
Ncos etc., armed forces				−0.0583 (6.06)
Security etc. service occupations				−0.0518 (16.08)
Catering occupations				−0.0345 (10.98)
Travel attendants etc. occupations				−0.0280 (4.06)
Health and related occupations				−0.0199 (5.10)
Childcare and related occupations				0.3007 (44.96)
Hairdressers, beauticians etc.				0.4172 (47.90)
Domestic staff etc.				−0.0347 (7.85)
Personal service occupations nes				0.0228 (3.79)
Buyers, brokers agents etc.				0.0591 (8.06)
Sales representatives				0.0942 (19.36)
Sales, check-out assistants				−0.0451 (17.96)
Mobile salespersons & agents				0.4964 (51.70)
Sales occupations nes				0.0884 (11.82)
Food, drink, tobacco operatives				−0.0367 (6.54)
Textiles, tannery operatives				0.0523 (5.02)
Chemicals, paper etc. operatives				−0.0233 (4.58)
Metal making, treating operatives				0.0099 (1.05)

Table A.10 (*Continued*).

	(1)	(2)	(3)	(4)
Metal working operatives				−0.0024 (0.40)
Assemblers, line workers				0.0086 (1.64)
Other routine operatives				−0.0465 (12.85)
Road transport operatives				0.1216 (25.24)
Other transport, machine operatives				0.0125 (2.89)
Plant & machine operatives nes				0.0819 (15.97)
Other farming related occupations				0.0687 (11.62)
Other manufacturing etc. occupations				0.0130 (1.61)
Other construction occupations				0.1986 (29.31)
Other transport occupations				−0.0349 (6.82)
Other communication occupations				0.0096 (2.18)
Other sales, service occupations				0.0027 (0.85)
Other occupations nes				−0.0002 (0.04)
Pseudo R^2	0.0663	0.0669	0.1822	0.3237
N	776,15	776,159	775,542	772,828

Source: Labor Force Surveys, 1994–1996.

Notes: Excluded categories; degree or equivalent; 1994; Gen managers – government, large orgs; Tyne and Wear. Dependent variable set to one if self-employed, zero if an employee.

Table A.11 Self-employment dprobits, 2004–2006.

	(1)	(2)	(3)	(4)
Age	0.0092 (43.66)	0.0092 (43.41)	0.0109 (55.19)	0.0073 (45.50)
Age^2	−0.00006 (26.12)	−0.00006 (25.85)	−0.0000 (35.85)	−0.00005 (27.85)
Male	0.0911 (110.09)	0.0912 (110.24)	0.0494 (60.52)	0.0166 (22.06)
Asian	0.0341 (14.39)	0.0139 (5.48)	0.0388 (15.62)	0.0315 (15.47)
Black	−0.0360 (11.41)	−0.0465 (15.01)	−0.0362 (12.61)	−0.0183 (7.89)
Chinese	0.0605 (8.02)	0.0348 (4.80)	0.0472 (6.97)	0.0322 (5.99)
Other race	0.0054 (1.31)	−0.0140 (3.43)	−0.0029 (0.75)	−0.0035 (1.17)
2005	−0.0013 (1.33)	−0.0013 (1.35)	−0.0018 (2.08)	−0.0015 (2.14)
2006	0.0006 (0.67)	0.0005 (0.50)	−0.0002 (0.31)	−0.0002 (0.38)
Immigrant		0.0282 (16.30)	0.0189 (11.98)	0.0092 (7.51)
Higher education	−0.0208 (13.95)	−0.0204 (13.64)	−0.0194 (14.19)	0.0015 (1.27)
GCSE A level or equiv.	0.0214 (17.79)	0.0224 (18.58)	−0.0080 (7.31)	0.0025 (2.61)
GCSE grades A–C or equiv.	−0.0089 (7.19)	−0.0076 (6.11)	−0.0267 (23.85)	0.0048 (4.54)
Other qualifications	−0.0095 (6.75)	−0.0120 (8.52)	−0.0322 (26.36)	−0.0054 (4.73)
No qualification	0.0070 (4.63)	0.0072 (4.73)	−0.0262 (20.06)	0.0012 (1.00)
Do not know	0.0243 (4.86)	0.0247 (4.93)	−0.0062 (1.48)	0.0158 (4.23)
Regions				
Rest of North			0.0238 (5.94)	0.0098 (3.18)
South Yorkshire			0.0173 (4.03)	0.0132 (3.84)
West Yorkshire			0.0237 (6.01)	0.0124 (4.04)
Rest Yorks & Humber			0.0393 (9.25)	0.0239 (7.11)
East Midlands			0.0365 (9.75)	0.0232 (7.80)
East Anglia			0.0393 (9.76)	0.0246 (7.69)
Inner London			0.0754 (16.85)	0.0398 (11.44)
Outer London			0.0563 (14.21)	0.0347 (11.01)
Rest of South East			0.0473 (13.54)	0.0300 (10.78)
South West			0.0525 (13.80)	0.0314 (10.40)

Table A.11 (*Continued*).

	(1)	(2)	(3)	(4)
West Midlands			0.0232 (5.91)	0.0155 (4.95)
Rest West Midlands			0.0455 (11.35)	0.0266 (8.42)
Greater Manchester			0.0272 (6.78)	0.0151 (4.79)
Merseyside			0.0088 (2.06)	0.0061 (1.78)
Rest of North West			0.0394 (9.70)	0.0245 (7.58)
Wales			0.0338 (8.59)	0.0202 (6.49)
Strathclyde			0.0002 (0.07)	−0.0029 (1.01)
Rest of Scotland			0.0151 (4.13)	0.0069 (2.42)
Northern Ireland			0.0795 (17.82)	0.0500 (13.95)
Industries				
Energy & water			−0.0944 (57.75)	−0.0593 (37.26)
Manufacturing			−0.1300 (103.97)	−0.0757 (49.66)
Construction			−0.0520 (25.93)	−0.0391 (18.15)
Distribution			−0.1231 (77.84)	−0.0612 (30.42)
Transport			−0.0991 (75.11)	−0.0547 (31.50)
Banking			−0.1062 (67.73)	−0.0480 (23.25)
Public administration			−0.1982 (111.89)	−0.1245 (60.94)
Other services			−0.0677 (36.88)	−0.0482 (27.44)
Workplace outside UK			−0.0859 (9.01)	−0.0452 (4.71)
Occupations				
Production managers				0.1299 (13.03)
Functional managers				0.0599 (7.49)
Quality and customer care managers				−0.0350 (4.63)
Financial instit and office manager				0.0116 (1.64)
Managers in distrib, storage and retail				0.1410 (13.72)
Protective service officers				−0.0011 (0.10)
Health and social services managers				0.1486 (12.38)
Managers in farming, hort, forestry etc.				0.3059 (17.79)

Table A.11 (*Continued*).

	(1)	(2)	(3)	(4)
Managers in hospitality and leisure				0.3655 (25.70)
Managers in other service industries				0.5311 (34.66)
Science professionals				0.0568 (5.42)
Engineering professionals				0.1457 (13.86)
Info & communication technology				0.1323 (12.95)
Health professionals				0.5993 (36.89)
Teaching professionals				0.1787 (16.57)
Research professionals				0.1567 (11.06)
Legal professionals				0.4107 (26.59)
Business & statistical professional				0.2453 (19.85)
Architects, town planners, surveyor				0.1885 (15.68)
Public service professionals				0.1070 (9.80)
Librarians and related professional				−0.0059 (0.50)
Science and engineering technician				0.0308 (3.59)
Draughtspersons & bldng inspectors				0.1567 (11.75)
IT service delivery occupations				0.0254 (2.87)
Health associate professionals				0.1130 (11.24)
Therapists				0.6494 (37.25)
Social welfare assoc. professionals				0.0942 (9.02)
Protective service occupations				−0.0311 (3.55)
Artistic and literary occupations				0.7805 (45.47)
Design associate professionals				0.5164 (31.13)
Media associate professionals				0.4567 (29.04)
Sports and fitness occupations				0.4666 (27.19)
Transport associate professionals				0.0265 (2.48)
Legal associate professionals				0.0749 (5.78)
Business & finance assoc. professnls				0.1703 (15.60)
Sales & related assoc. professionals				0.1714 (15.53)
Conservation associate professional				0.0836 (5.53)

Table A.11 (*Continued*).

	(1)	(2)	(3)	(4)
Public service and other assoc. profs				0.1313 (12.70)
Administrative: government & relate				−0.0438 (6.87)
Administrative occupations: finance				0.0368 (4.86)
Administrative occupations: records				−0.0084 (1.32)
Administrative: communications				−0.0196 (1.61)
Administrative occupations: general				0.0273 (3.65)
Secretarial and related occupations				0.0237 (3.29)
Agricultural trades				0.4719 (29.94)
Metal forming, welding and related				0.2196 (16.46)
Metal machining, fitting, instr. making				0.0856 (9.03)
Vehicle trades				0.2092 (17.24)
Electrical trades				0.2091 (17.86)
Construction trades				0.5165 (34.13)
Building trades				0.6314 (37.74)
Textiles and garment trades				0.5335 (28.03)
Painting trades				0.1586 (11.59)
Food preparation trades				0.1409 (13.01)
Skilled trades n.e.c				0.5139 (30.38)
Healthcare & related personal service				0.0880 (9.44)
Childcare & related personal services				0.3663 (26.25)
Animal care services				0.2337 (13.56)
Leisure & travel service				0.0682 (6.82)
Hairdressers and related				0.5850 (34.97)
Housekeeping occupations				−0.0147 (1.83)
Personal services occupations n.e.c				0.1577 (8.88)
Sales assistants and retail cashier				−0.0233 (4.27)
Sales related				0.3254 (23.29)

Table A.11 (*Continued*).

	(1)	(2)	(3)	(4)
Customer service				−0.0412 (7.10)
Process operatives				0.0090 (1.16)
Print and machine operatives				0.0467 (4.98)
Assemblers and routine operatives				0.0614 (6.74)
Construction operatives				0.1710 (14.40)
Transport drivers and operatives				0.2668 (21.75)
Mobile machine drivers & operatives				0.0005 (0.08)
Elementary agricultural				0.0788 (7.40)
Elementary construction				0.2615 (19.92)
Elementary process plant				−0.0085 (1.14)
Elementary goods storage				−0.0404 (7.44)
Elementary administration				0.0244 (3.04)
Elementary personal service				−0.0201 (3.35)
Elementary cleaning				0.1462 (14.21)
Elementary security				−0.0209 (3.29)
Elementary sales				−0.0535 (7.51)
Pseudo R^2	0.0653	0.0674	0.1652	0.3061
N	632,982	632,917	632,415	632,218

Source: Labor Force Surveys, 2004–2006.

Notes: Excluded categories; degree or equivalent; 2004; Corporate managers & senior officials; Tyne and Wear. T-statistics in parentheses.

Table A.12 Second job self-employment, dprobits, 2004–2006.

	(1)	(2)	(3)
Age	0.0012 (17.46)	0.0010 (14.86)	0.0008 (12.22)
Age^2	−0.00001 (15.00)	−0.00001 (13.03)	−0.00001 (9.61)
Male	0.0008 (3.13)	0.0024 (9.76)	0.0016 (6.77)
Asian	−0.0029 (3.63)	−0.0026 (3.46)	−0.0025 (3.65)
Black	−0.0041 (4.43)	−0.0042 (4.80)	−0.0035 (4.19)
Chinese	−0.0005 (0.24)	−0.0011 (0.55)	−0.0018 (1.01)
Other race	0.0008 (0.66)	0.0004 (0.34)	0.0005 (0.45)
2005	0.0000 (0.06)	0.0000 (0.07)	−0.0000 (0.15)
2006	0.0000 (0.13)	0.0000 (0.12)	−0.0001 (0.59)
Immigrant	−0.0005 (1.11)	−0.0007 (1.53)	−0.0003 (0.84)
Rest of North	0.0034 (2.20)	0.0034 (2.27)	0.0031 (2.22)
South Yorkshire	0.0034 (2.02)	0.0031 (1.95)	0.0031 (2.06)
West Yorkshire	0.0068 (4.10)	0.0068 (4.25)	0.0063 (4.20)
Rest Yorks & Humber	0.0027 (1.73)	0.0031 (2.04)	0.0029 (2.07)
East Midlands	0.0069 (4.47)	0.0072 (4.83)	0.0065 (4.66)
East Anglia	0.0116 (6.40)	0.0115 (6.50)	0.0104 (6.32)
Inner London	0.0150 (7.39)	0.0147 (7.47)	0.0100 (5.92)
Outer London	0.0067 (4.27)	0.0068 (4.44)	0.0049 (3.58)
Rest of South East	0.0094 (6.45)	0.0097 (6.83)	0.0079 (6.12)
South West	0.0111 (6.70)	0.0115 (7.05)	0.0098 (6.54)
West Midlands	0.0040 (2.59)	0.0039 (2.65)	0.0036 (2.57)
Rest West Midlands	0.0051 (3.29)	0.0056 (3.70)	0.0048 (3.45)
Greater Manchester	0.0047 (2.98)	0.0048 (3.12)	0.0041 (2.88)
Merseyside	−0.0030 (2.07)	−0.0029 (2.13)	−0.0024 (1.88)
Rest of North West	0.0054 (3.41)	0.0060 (3.83)	0.0051 (3.53)
Wales	0.0049 (3.18)	0.0045 (3.10)	0.0041 (3.01)
Strathclyde	−0.0003 (0.27)	−0.0004 (0.34)	−0.0003 (0.31)
Rest of Scotland	0.0076 (4.73)	0.0071 (4.64)	0.0064 (4.46)
Northern Ireland	0.0080 (4.63)	0.0072 (4.40)	0.0072 (4.61)
Public company, plc		−0.0011 (1.35)	−0.0017 (2.21)
Nationalized industry etc.		−0.0023 (1.64)	−0.0022 (1.65)
Central govt, civil service		0.0012 (1.78)	−0.0009 (1.56)
Local govt or council		0.0060 (14.97)	0.0023 (6.76)
University, etc.		0.0229 (20.51)	0.0100 (11.71)
Health authority/NHS trust		0.0117 (19.74)	0.0075 (13.96)
Charity, voluntary org. etc.		0.0191 (19.89)	0.0120 (14.98)
Armed forces		−0.0059 (3.79)	−0.0055 (3.99)
Other public organization		0.0033 (2.22)	0.0003 (0.30)
Higher degree			0.0325 (23.05)
NVQ level 5			0.0315 (6.94)
First/Foundation degree			0.0216 (20.00)
Other degree			0.0307 (14.77)
NVQ level 4			0.0168 (7.36)
Diploma in higher Educn			0.0221 (12.25)
HNC, HND, BTEC etc. higher			0.0183 (14.11)
Teaching, further educn			0.0408 (11.05)
Teaching, secondary educn			0.0019 (0.62)

Table A.12 (*Continued*).

	(1)	(2)	(3)
Teaching, primary educn			0.0232 (7.57)
Teaching foundation stage			0.0278 (2.98)
Teaching, level not stated			0.0408 (6.89)
Nursing etc.			0.0083 (6.27)
RSA higher diploma			0.0088 (1.35)
Other Higher Educn below degree			0.0321 (11.15)
NVQ level 3			0.0133 (10.12)
International bac'te			0.0416 (3.23)
GNVQ/GSVQ advanced			0.0203 (6.37)
A level or equivalent			0.0174 (14.89)
RSA advanced diploma			0.0246 (4.36)
OND, ONC, BTEC etc., national			0.0157 (9.87)
City & guilds advanced craft/part 1			0.0061 (4.96)
SCE higher or equivalent			0.0106 (4.84)
Access qualifications			0.0152 (2.19)
A,S level or equivalent			0.0118 (3.86)
Trade apprenticeship			0.0063 (6.41)
NVQ level 2 or equivalent			0.0103 (8.04)
Intermediate Welsh bac'te			0.0107 (1.68)
GNVQ/GSVQ intermediate			0.0028 (0.61)
RSA diploma			0.0139 (2.91)
City & Guilds craft/part 2			0.0153 (7.14)
BTEC, SCOTVEC first diploma etc.			0.0190 (4.45)
O level, GCSE grade a–c or equiv.			0.0091 (11.05)
NVQ level 1 or equivalent			−0.0007 (0.30)
CSE below grade1, gcse < grade c			0.0060 (4.82)
RSA other			0.0075 (3.65)
City & guilds foundation/part 1			0.0028 (0.73)
YT, YTP certificate			0.0084 (0.79)
Key skills qualification			0.0005 (0.08)
Other qualification			0.0062 (6.60)
Do not know			−0.0023 (1.01)
Pseudo R^2	0.0162	0.0323	0.0518
N	551,584	550,131	548,659

Source: Labor Force Surveys, 2004–2006.

Notes: Sample consists of employees in their first jobs. Dependent variable set to one if employed in first job and self-employed in second job and 0 otherwise. Excluded – Tyne and Wear; whites; no qualification and private sector.

Table A.13 US Self-employment rates – incorporated and unincorporated, 2005.

	Unincorporated self-employed			Incorporated self-employed			Wage/salary workers		
	Total	Male	Female	Total	Male	Female	Total	Male	Female
Total (1,000)	10,464	6,632	3,832	5,254	3,828	1,425	125,889	65,467	60,423
% employment	7.4%	8.7%	5.8%	3.7%	5.0%	2.2%			
16–19 years old	0.8	0.8	0.6	0.1	0.1	0.1	4.7	4.4	5.0
20–24 years old	3.0	3.3	2.4	1.1	1.0	1.4	10.7	10.7	10.6
25–34 years old	15.4	14.9	16.2	11.6	11.5	11.8	22.6	23.8	21.3
35–44 years old	24.4	23.7	25.7	26.6	26.3	27.3	24.4	24.7	23.9
45–54 years old	26.9	27.2	26.5	31.4	31.4	31.6	22.8	22.0	23.6
55–64 years old	19.8	19.5	20.3	20.9	21.2	20.1	12.0	11.6	12.5
65 years old+	9.7	10.6	8.2	8.2	8.4	7.6	2.9	2.8	3.0
White	87.6	87.9	87.2	89.7	90.3	88.0	81.8	83.2	80.3
Black	6.3	6.3	6.1	3.7	3.4	4.6	11.5	10.1	13.0
Asian	4.1	3.8	4.6	5.3	5.0	6.0	4.4	4.4	4.3
Hispanic	9.9	11.2	7.6	6.2	6.2	6.2	13.7	15.8	11.4
US born	86.6	85.5	88.3	86.6	86.8	86.2	85.0	82.8	87.4
Foreign-born	13.7	14.7	12.0	13.4	13.2	13.9	15.0	17.2	12.6
US citizen	6.2	6.2	6.1	8.7	8.7	8.8	5.9	5.8	5.9
Not US citizen	7.5	8.5	5.8	4.6	4.5	5.0	9.1	11.3	6.7

Source: Current Population Survey. 2007 Statistical Abstract of the US, Table 590. Downloadable at www.census.gov/compendia.
statab/tables/07s0590.xls.
Notes: Wage and salary workers excludes the incorporated self-employed.

Table A.14 US Self-employment (incorporated+unincorporated) dprobits, 2004–2006.

	(1)	(2)	(3)	(4)
Age	0.0094 (53.62)	0.0093 (53.17)	0.0104 (60.99)	0.0087 (56.44)
Age^2	−0.00007 (32.68)	−0.00006 (32.27)	−0.00007 (40.17)	−0.00006 (37.17)
Male	0.0515 (78.29)	0.0514 (78.23)	0.0256 (39.31)	0.0236 (37.07)
Asian	−0.0130 (6.83)	−0.0207 (9.81)	−0.0151 (6.93)	−0.0094 (4.69)
Black	−0.0543 (43.67)	−0.0549 (43.56)	−0.0375 (28.72)	−0.0298 (26.33)
Native American	−0.0300 (7.15)	−0.0300 (7.18)	−0.0272 (6.84)	−0.0213 (6.03)
Hispanic	−0.0303 (22.19)	−0.0349 (24.68)	−0.0361 (25.95)	−0.0275 (22.78)
Other race	−0.0069 (2.20)	−0.0073 (2.33)	−0.0088 (2.82)	−0.0053 (1.88)
2005	−0.0017 (1.45)	−0.0017 (1.45)	−0.0019 (1.64)	−0.0017 (1.72)
2006	−0.0012 (1.07)	−0.0013 (1.12)	−0.0021 (1.85)	−0.0025 (2.51)
Immigrant		0.0130 (8.36)	0.0078 (5.41)	0.0079 (6.20)
1st–4th grade	−0.0110 (0.93)	−0.0113 (0.96)	−0.0123 (1.05)	−0.0124 (1.27)
5th or 6th grade	0.0160 (1.28)	0.0157 (1.27)	0.0145 (1.16)	0.0092 (0.88)
7th or 8th grade	0.0486 (3.72)	0.0525 (3.98)	0.0687 (4.80)	0.0469 (3.92)
9th grade	0.0263 (1.96)	0.0303 (2.23)	0.0501 (3.51)	0.0306 (2.57)
10th grade	0.0352 (2.65)	0.0413 (3.05)	0.0692 (4.68)	0.0439 (3.58)
11th grade	0.0210 (1.67)	0.0270 (2.10)	0.0574 (4.08)	0.0328 (2.86)
12th grade no diploma	0.0181 (1.41)	0.0230 (1.76)	0.0520 (3.68)	0.0267 (2.31)
High school graduate	0.0237 (1.96)	0.0292 (2.38)	0.0610 (4.75)	0.0355 (3.30)
Some college	0.0353 (2.82)	0.0415 (3.26)	0.0833 (6.00)	0.0474 (4.18)
Associates – vocational	0.0287 (2.27)	0.0349 (2.71)	0.0794 (5.44)	0.0412 (3.58)
Associates – academic	0.0163 (1.35)	0.0222 (1.80)	0.0785 (5.42)	0.0410 (3.52)
Bachelor's degree	0.0372 (2.94)	0.0430 (3.34)	0.0986 (6.83)	0.0510 (4.40)
Master's degree	0.0056 (0.46)	0.0105 (0.85)	0.0841 (5.54)	0.0507 (4.05)
Professional degree	0.1532 (8.72)	0.1618 (9.09)	0.2891 (13.31)	0.2476 (12.80)
Doctorate degree	0.0657 (4.35)	0.0716 (4.66)	0.2030 (10.26)	0.1801 (10.06)
States				
Alabama			−0.0230 (5.91)	−0.0210 (6.07)
Alaska			0.0045 (1.20)	0.0063 (1.85)
Arizona			−0.0104 (2.68)	−0.0161 (4.87)
Arkansas			−0.0055 (1.39)	−0.0056 (1.59)

Table A.14 (Continued).

	(1)	(2)	(3)	(4)
California			0.0146 (5.26)	0.0043 (1.79)
Colorado			0.0081 (2.22)	0.0001 (0.03)
Connecticut			-0.0200 (6.76)	-0.0215 (8.46)
District of Columbia			-0.0269 (7.28)	-0.0310 (9.84)
Delaware			-0.0303 (8.31)	-0.0287 (9.03)
Florida			-0.0036 (1.35)	-0.0092 (3.95)
Georgia			-0.0097 (2.96)	-0.0128 (4.53)
Hawaii			-0.0115 (2.89)	-0.0147 (4.30)
Idaho			0.0099 (2.26)	0.0082 (2.08)
Illinois			-0.0226 (8.16)	-0.0241 (9.97)
Indiana			-0.0225 (6.85)	-0.0226 (7.91)
Iowa			-0.0110 (3.43)	-0.0145 (4.99)
Kansas			-0.0039 (1.06)	-0.0072 (2.18)
Kentucky			-0.0242 (7.00)	-0.0232 (7.72)
Louisiana			-0.0102 (2.39)	-0.0123 (3.47)
Maryland			-0.0222 (7.52)	-0.0242 (9.85)
Massachusetts			-0.0241 (7.47)	-0.0236 (8.55)
Michigan			-0.0160 (5.06)	-0.0172 (6.33)
Minnesota			-0.0078 (2.43)	-0.0117 (4.24)
Mississippi			-0.0052 (1.18)	-0.0067 (1.73)
Missouri			-0.0165 (4.92)	-0.0169 (5.83)
Montana			0.0161 (3.96)	0.0121 (3.26)
Nebraska			-0.0147 (4.14)	-0.0167 (5.33)
Nevada			-0.0237 (6.70)	-0.0277 (9.23)
New Hampshire			-0.0088 (2.92)	-0.0102 (3.81)
New Jersey			-0.0228 (7.52)	-0.0233 (9.09)
New Mexico			0.0036 (0.68)	-0.0033 (0.76)
New York			-0.0138 (5.03)	-0.0175 (7.34)
North Carolina			-0.0173 (5.03)	-0.0183 (6.19)

Table A.14 (*Continued*).

	(1)	(2)	(3)	(4)
North Dakota			-0.0057 (1.60)	-0.0122 (3.97)
Ohio			-0.0243 (8.06)	-0.0235 (9.15)
Oklahoma			0.0068 (1.60)	0.0020 (0.54)
Oregon			0.0067 (1.84)	0.0004 (0.15)
Pennsylvania			-0.0267 (9.58)	-0.0252 (10.38)
Rhode Island			-0.0222 (7.41)	-0.0219 (8.48)
South Carolina			-0.0156 (4.06)	-0.0166 (4.89)
South Dakota			0.0053 (1.54)	-0.0023 (0.77)
Tennessee			-0.0094 (2.42)	-0.0124 (3.73)
Texas			-0.0045 (1.61)	-0.0090 (3.61)
Utah			0.0092 (2.40)	0.0032 (0.94)
Vermont			0.0051 (1.44)	0.0019 (0.63)
Virginia			-0.0221 (7.07)	-0.0242 (9.18)
Washington			-0.0130 (3.82)	-0.0139 (4.69)
West Virginia			-0.0355 (10.21)	-0.0317 (10.30)
Wisconsin			-0.0088 (2.35)	-0.0109 (3.39)
Wyoming			0.0053 (1.33)	0.0008 (0.25)
Mining			-0.0848 (42.80)	-0.0693 (43.87)
Industries				
Construction			-0.0689 (46.74)	-0.0686 (46.91)
Manufacturing			-0.1200 (115.41)	-0.1046 (100.68)
Wholesale and Retail Trade			-0.1116 (90.39)	-0.1097 (92.54)
Transportation and Utilities			-0.0933 (82.66)	-0.0778 (77.00)
Information			-0.0879 (76.17)	-0.0744 (84.12)
Financial Activities			-0.0911 (82.70)	-0.0822 (84.42)
Professional & Business Services			-0.0824 (59.05)	-0.0750 (54.96)
Educational & Health Services			-0.1519 (114.22)	-0.1405 (95.87)
Leisure and hospitality			-0.0950 (75.46)	-0.0864 (72.63)
Other Services			-0.0745 (53.80)	-0.0731 (64.52)

Table A.14 (*Continued*).

	(1)	(2)	(3)	(4)
Occupations				
Business and financial operations				-0.0392 (30.81)
Computer and mathematical science				-0.0613 (47.11)
Architecture and engineering				-0.0625 (45.51)
Life, physical & social science				-0.0519 (21.70)
Community and social service				-0.0620 (30.59)
Legal occupations				-0.0544 (33.31)
Education, training, and library				-0.0628 (46.49)
Arts, design, entertainment, sports, & media				0.0681 (27.57)
Healthcare practitioner and technical				-0.0393 (28.06)
Healthcare support				-0.0407 (18.82)
Protective service				-0.0678 (31.70)
Food preparation and serving related				-0.0664 (49.03)
Building & grounds cleaning & maintenance				-0.0364 (26.94)
Personal care and service				0.0930 (38.55)
Sales and related				0.0080 (5.56)
Office & administrative support				-0.0731 (80.93)
Farming, fishing, & forestry				-0.0690 (53.28)
Construction & extraction				-0.0422 (33.87)
Installation, maintenance & repair				-0.0477 (39.88)
Production occupations				-0.0502 (40.19)
Transportation & material moving				-0.0529 (48.30)
Pseudo R^2	0.0654	0.0656	0.1548	0.1642
N	2,254,528	2,254,528	2,144,356	2,144,356

Source: Basic Monthly files of the Current Population Survey, 2004–2006.

Notes: Excluded categories: Whites; Less than 1st grade; Maine; Agriculture, Forestry, Fishing and Hunting; Management occupations. Public administration is dropped in columns 3 and 4 as all workers are employees. Standard errors are adjusted for clustering at the household level. Incorporated sample excludes the unincorporated self-employed while the unincorporated sample excludes the incorporated self-employed. Ages 16–70.

Table A.15 European Union self-employment dprobits.

	1974–2002	2005–2006
Time	−0.0016 (22.71)	n/a
Age	0.0052 (20.85)	0.0060 (4.06)
Age^2	0.00001 (0.48)	−0.00002 (1.47)
Male	0.0529 (46.98)	0.0613 (10.09)
Austria	0.0716 (17.51)	−0.0008 (0.04)
Belgium	0.0883 (29.11)	0.0173 (0.76)
Bulgaria		−0.0014 (0.06)
Croatia		0.0296 (1.19)
Cyprus Republic		0.0117 (0.44)
Cyprus Turkish		0.4431 (12.58)
Czech Republic		0.0780 (3.33)
Denmark	−0.0278 (10.33)	−0.0136 (0.63)
East Germany	−0.0089 (2.59)	0.1045 (3.37)
Estonia		0.0180 (0.78)
Finland	0.0500 (11.60)	−0.0094 (0.44)
France	0.0453 (15.74)	−0.0302 (1.42)
Greece	0.3557 (97.56)	0.3128 (10.88)
Hungary		−0.0043 (0.19)
Ireland	0.1727 (54.05)	0.0366 (1.61)
Italy	0.1877 (58.20)	0.1661 (6.61)
Latvia		−0.0531 (2.56)
Lithuania		−0.0372 (1.65)
Luxembourg	0.0124 (3.36)	−0.0005 (0.02)
Malta		−0.0001 (0.00)
Netherlands	0.0056 (1.90)	−0.0293 (1.46)
Norway	0.0094 (1.65)	n/a
Poland		0.1326 (4.77)
Portugal	0.1398 (39.70)	0.0277 (1.13)
Romania		0.0726 (2.93)
Slovakia		0.0219 (1.00)
Slovenia		0.0217 (0.92)
Spain	0.1434 (39.32)	−0.0329 (1.35)
Sweden	−0.0158 (4.08)	0.0026 (0.13)
Turkey		0.4608 (14.15)
West Germany	0.0013 (0.51)	0.0248 (1.12)
Age left school 15	−0.0333 (15.43)	
Age left school 16	−0.0320 (15.85)	
Age left school 17	−0.0311 (14.06)	
Age left school 18	−0.0308 (15.91)	
Age left school 19	−0.0281 (11.63)	
Age left school 20	−0.0317 (12.31)	

Table A.15 (*Continued*).

	1974–2002	2005–2006
Age left school 21	−0.0341 (12.10)	
Age left school ≥22	−0.0188 (10.26)	
Still studying	−0.0460 (5.94)	
Age left school 16–19		−0.0260 (2.82)
Age left school 20+		−0.0284 (2.97)
No schooling		−0.0240 (0.53)
Pseudo R^2	0.0982	0.1084
N	488,548	13,769

Sources: Column 1: Eurobarometer Trend file 1975–2002 (ICPSR #4357); Column 2: Euro-barometer 64.4, Mental well-being, Telecommunications, Harmful Internet Content and Farm Animal welfare, December 2005–January 2006 (ICPSR #4667).
Notes: Column 1: Excluded category UK and Age left school at 14 or under; Column 2: Excluded category UK and Age left school at 15 or under. T-statistics in parentheses.

Table A.16 Desire for self-employment and difficulties in starting a business (workers only).

	(1)	(2)	(3)	(4)
Austria		40	39	32
Belgium	37	29	31	
Cyprus		59	39	18
Czech Republic	39	37	39	33
Denmark	30	36	24	37
Estonia		49	47	43
Finland		28	17	27
France	42	43	38	41
Germany		46	32	34
Greece		63	51	37
Hungary	50	47	58	46
Iceland		61	22	15
Ireland		62	21	18
Italy	63	57	32	31
Latvia		44	48	41
Lichtenstein		54	20	10
Lithuania		62	52	58
Luxembourg		45	30	27
Malta		46	52	28
Netherlands	36	33	9	16
Norway	27	36	14	25
Poland	80	57	42	37
Portugal	73	69	36	34

Table A.16 (*Continued*).

	(1)	(2)	(3)	(4)
Slovakia		36	33	28
Slovenia	58	35	62	61
Spain	39	61	35	26
Sweden	39	35	39	45
UK	45	47	24	24
USA	71	66	26	20

Sources: Column 1 1997/1998 International Social Survey Programme and Blanch-flower et al. (2001). Columns 2–4 Flash Eurobarometers 160 Entrepreneurship 5, 2004; Flash Eurobarometer 146 Entrepreneurship 4, 2003; Flash Eurobarometer 134 Entrepreneurship 3, 2002; Flash Eurobarometer 107 Entrepreneurship 2, 2001; Flash Eurobarometer 83 Entrepreneurship 1, 2000. ZUMA German Archive ZA #4184; 4156; 3772; 3596 and 3498 (GESIS/ZA Central Archive for Empirical Social Research) http://www.gesis.org/eurobarometer.

Notes: Columns 1 and 2. Suppose you were working and could choose between different kinds of work. Which would you prefer being an employee or self-employed – tabulated here is % saying prefer being self-employed.

Column 3 – do you strongly agree, agree, disagree, strongly disagree with the following opinion – it is difficult to start one's own business due to a lack of available financial support – tabulated here is the % who strongly agree.

Column 4 – do you strongly agree, agree, disagree, strongly disagree with the following opinion – it is difficult to start one's own business due to the complex administrative procedures – tabulated here is the % who strongly agree.

Table A.17 Probabilities of being self-employed, dprobit, NCDS7 2004/2005.

	(1)	(2)	(3)	(4)
Male	0.1150 (13.67)	0.1140 (13.54)	0.1082 (12.17)	0.1073 (13.57)
Gift (1981/£1000)	0.0038 (3.30)	0.0036 (3.19)	0.0030 (2.54)	0.0027 (2.57)
North		−0.0230 (1.03)	−0.0307 (1.32)	−0.0255 (1.25)
Yorks & Humberside		0.0147 (0.70)	0.0040 (0.19)	0.0035 (0.19)
East Midlands		0.0258 (1.20)	0.0154 (0.70)	0.0191 (0.97)
East Anglia		0.0477 (1.82)	0.0367 (1.39)	0.0376 (1.60)
South East		0.0592 (3.47)	0.0476 (2.69)	0.0456 (2.92)
South West		0.0577 (2.71)	0.0453 (2.08)	0.0443 (2.29)
West Midlands		0.0186 (0.90)	0.0101 (0.47)	0.0113 (0.61)
North West		−0.0082 (0.42)	−0.0182 (0.88)	−0.0133 (0.73)
Wales		0.0293 (1.21)	0.0033 (0.14)	0.0014 (0.07)
CSEs 2–5		−0.0084 (0.58)	−0.0052 (0.34)	0.0114 (0.82)
GCSE O levels		−0.0016 (0.14)	−0.0085 (0.64)	0.0098 (0.85)
AS levels		−0.0718 (1.21)	−0.0979 (1.54)	−0.0784 (1.34)
2+ A-levels		−0.0134 (0.80)	−0.0208 (1.18)	−0.0020 (0.13)
Diploma		−0.0199 (0.91)	−0.0316 (1.40)	−0.0106 (0.51)
Degree		−0.0104 (0.73)	−0.0228 (1.50)	−0.0002 (0.02)
Higher degree		−0.0274 (1.19)	−0.0305 (1.24)	−0.0076 (0.33)
Copying design test			0.0103 (3.22)	0.0087 (3.14)
Father's social class in 1969				
Manager employing < 25			0.0555 (3.78)	0.0530 (4.03)
Professional – self-employed			0.0594 (1.33)	0.0513 (1.30)
Worker own-account			0.0970 (3.45)	0.0804 (3.29)
Farmer employer manager			0.1990 (4.37)	0.1863 (4.51)
Farmer own account			0.2276 (4.26)	0.2252 (4.55)
Workers only	Yes	Yes	Yes	No
Pseudo R^2	0.0333	0.0404	0.0520	0.0582
N	7,216	7,214	6,325	7,188

Source: NCDS.

Notes: Excluded categories; no qualifications; Scotland and ten other labour market statuses from 1969 when the respondent was aged 11. T-statistics in parentheses.

Copying Designs Test Score: For age 11.

To obtain some assessment of the child's perceptuo-motor ability. The child, on a specially designed form, is asked to make two attempts to copy each of six different shapes. A score of 0 or 1 is allocated for each attempt. The total score range is 0–12.

Table A.18 Self-employment rates and house prices (in logs).

	(1)	(2)	(3)	(4)	(5)
Log house prices$_t$	0.2742 (6.68)	0.0434 (2.59)	0.1318 (3.25)	0.0952 (2.64)	0.1237 (5.77)
Log unemployment rate$_t$	−0.1298 (2.95)	0.0062 (0.37)	0.0842 (2.27)	0.0310 (0.92)	0.1955 (7.18)
Log self-employment rate$_{t-1}$		0.9196 (36.53)		0.4440 (7.05)	0.5607 (11.63)
Price deflator					−0.0001 (1.21)
East Midlands			−0.1502 (8.62)	−0.0769 (4.18)	−0.0778 (3.65)
London			−0.0395 (1.17)	−0.0134 (0.44)	−0.1099 (4.23)
Northern Ireland			0.0920 (3.95)	0.0798 (3.79)	−0.0082 (0.38)
North East			−0.3498 (14.28)	−0.1779 (5.58)	−0.2228 (6.76)
North West			−0.2021 (10.33)	−0.1063 (4.87)	−0.1297 (5.33)
Scotland			−0.3231 (15.29)	−0.1631 (5.77)	−0.1861 (6.33)
South East			−0.0085 (0.44)	−0.0115 (0.67)	−0.0092 (0.47)
South West			0.1201 (7.22)	0.0572 (3.38)	0.0397 (2.00)
Wales			−0.0415 (2.08)	−0.0181 (1.02)	−0.0631 (3.01)
West Midlands			−0.2097 (10.60)	−0.1042 (4.69)	−0.1336 (5.56)
Yorks & Humberside			−0.1934 (9.95)	−0.1006 (4.66)	−0.1209 (5.01)
1987	0.0418 (0.72)	0.0739 (2.44)	0.0624 (2.81)	0.0799 (1.72)	
1988	−0.0240 (0.41)	0.0101 (0.36)	0.0674 (2.77)	0.0474 (1.15)	
1989	−0.0401 (0.66)	0.0423 (1.58)	0.1085 (3.92)	0.0808 (2.19)	
1990	−0.0517 (0.85)	−0.0181 (0.66)	0.1003 (3.65)	0.0470 (1.24)	
1991	−0.0407 (0.68)	−0.0203 (0.74)	0.0711 (2.61)	0.0338 (0.91)	
1992	0.1326 (2.15)	0.1619 (5.79)	0.2398 (8.64)	0.2133 (5.65)	
1993	0.1393 (2.27)	0.0022 (0.07)	0.2371 (8.62)	0.1354 (3.34)	
1994	0.1674 (2.80)	0.0300 (1.01)	0.2571 (9.75)	0.1638 (4.04)	
1995	0.0665 (1.11)	−0.0799 (2.68)	0.1765 (6.80)	0.0594 (1.44)	
1996	0.0169 (0.28)	−0.0290 (1.03)	0.1462 (5.46)	0.0671 (1.73)	

Table A.18 (*Continued*).

	(1)	(2)	(3)	(4)	(5)
1997	−0.0605 (0.99)	−0.0425 (1.56)	0.1104 (3.85)	0.0393 (1.05)	
1998	−0.1340 (2.13)	−0.0514 (1.96)	0.0678 (2.21)	0.0110 (0.30)	
1999	−0.1755 (2.75)	−0.0324 (1.27)	0.0441 (1.37)	0.0070 (0.20)	
2000	−0.2427 (3.70)	−0.0475 (1.92)	0.0125 (0.36)	−0.0189 (0.58)	
2001	−0.2807 (4.17)	−0.0311 (1.30)	0.0004 (0.01)	−0.0188 (0.61)	
2002	−0.3228 (4.65)	−0.0301 (1.32)	−0.0185 (0.45)	−0.0290 (1.10)	
2003	−0.3314 (4.54)	0.0093 (0.42)	0.0099 (0.21)	0.0028 (0.13)	
2004	−0.3841 (4.99)	−0.0401 (1.86)	−0.0045 (0.09)	−0.0305 (1.51)	
2005	−0.4021 (5.15)	−0.0500 (2.33)	−0.0173 (0.32)	−0.0420 (2.16)	
2006	−0.3630 (4.55)		0.0157 (0.28)		
Constant	−0.1291 (0.26)	0.2684 (1.12)	0.9604 (2.02)	0.3206 (0.68)	−0.4877 (1.77)
Adjusted R^2	0.3688	0.9118	0.9227	0.9413	0.8949
N	250	237	250	237	237

Source: Labor Force Survey and Nationwide data on house prices. T-statistics in parentheses.

Table A.19 Growth rates in real GDP regressions, 1967–2005.

	(1)	(2)	(3)	(4)
$\text{Self}_t - \text{Self}_{t-1}$	−0.0602	0.0180		
	(0.76)	(0.23)		
$\text{Self}_t - \text{Self}_{t-1}$			−0.3089	−0.1672
(Non-agricultural)			(2.16)	(1.20)
GDP_{t-1}	0.2705	0.2187	0.2650	0.2159
	(8.24)	(6.74)	(7.98)	(6.57)
$\text{Emp}_t - \text{Emp}_{t-1}$		0.0014		0.0013
		(7.58)		(7.26)
N	845	845	820	820
Adjusted R^2	0.2115	0.2628	0.2429	0.2429
F	8.30	10.40	7.54	9.48

Source: OECD Labour Force Statistics and OECD National Accounts.

Notes: Columns (1) & (2) include 29 country dummies. Countries are: Australia, Austria, Belgium, Canada, Czech, Denmark, Finland, France, Germany, Greece, Hungary, Iceland, Ireland, Italy, Japan, South Korea, Luxembourg, Mexico, Netherlands, New Zealand, Norway, Poland, Portugal, Slovakia, Spain, Sweden, Switzerland, Turkey, UK and USA. Column (3) & (4) include 28 country dummies. Data for Switzerland are not available. T-statistics in parentheses.

Self-employment is defined as all self-employed over total employment in columns 1 and 2 and as non-agricultural self-employed over total non-agricultural employment in columns 3 and 4. Employment is total numbers of employees.

Dependent variable = real GDP growth rate.

Table A.20 Life satisfaction ordered logits.

	Eurobarometer Europe 1970–2002	Eurobarometer UK 1970–2002	BHPS UK 2004/2005
Age	−0.0456 (45.34)	−0.0314 (11.00)	−0.0444 (7.22)
Age^2	0.0005 (47.49)	0.0004 (14.69)	0.0005 (8.38)
Male	−0.1150 (19.82)	−0.1722 (9.99)	−0.0235 (0.73)
Time trend	0.0058 (15.17)	0.0065 (6.16)	n/a
Married	0.3413 (44.89)	0.2940 (12.65)	0.3469 (7.44)
Divorced	−0.4868 (31.55)	−0.6660 (14.82)	−0.1945 (2.84)
Separated	−0.6379 (26.04)	−0.6492 (10.40)	−0.4184 (3.77)
Widowed	−0.2791 (21.91)	−0.3464 (9.18)	−0.1918 (2.33)
Self-employed	0.0422 (4.49)	0.0844 (2.59)	0.1296 (2.15)
Unemployed	−0.9842 (84.45)	−1.0764 (32.33)	−0.6635 (6.94)
Retired	−0.0475 (4.59)	−0.1084 (3.60)	0.0134 (0.20)
Maternity leave			0.4905 (2.58)
Family care	−0.0276 (3.19)	−0.1218 (5.19)	−0.2003 (2.95)
Student	0.2256 (10.21)	0.1661 (2.19)	0.0905 (1.14)
LT Sick/disabled			−1.5882 (19.52)
Govt scheme			0.3711 (1.15)
Other	−0.0281 (1.38)	0.0117 (0.19)	−0.4059 (1.98)
Schooling dummies	11	11	14
Region dummies	–	–	18
Country dummies	16	–	–
Cut1	−4.2851	−3.5599	−5.2809
Cut2	−2.5937	−2.0856	−4.2023
Cut3	0.3094	0.6933	−3.0939
Cut4			−2.0203
Cut5			−0.6628
Cut6			1.0916
Pseudo R^2	0.0818	0.0250	0.0211
N	598,116	66,339	14,232

Notes: Austria, Belgium, Denmark, East Germany, Finland, France, Greece, Ireland, Italy, Luxembourg, Netherlands, Norway, Portugal, Spain, Sweden, West Germany.

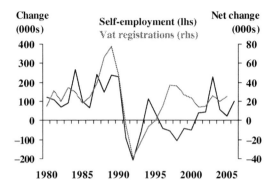

Correlation, 1980–2005: +0.60

Source: DTI & ONS

Chart A.1 Net change in VAT registrations and change in self-employment.

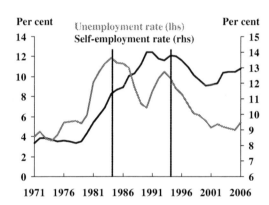

Correlation, 1971–2006: +0.41

Correlation, 1984–1994: −0.75

Source: ONS

Chart A.2 Unemployment rate and self-employment rate.

Correlation, 1971–2006: –0.33

Correlation, 1984–1994: +0.72

Source: ONS

Chart A.3 Employment rate and self-employment rate.

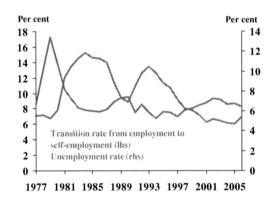

Correlation since 1977: –0.38

Source: ONS & Labour Force Survey microdata Spring quarters

Chart A.4 Rate of transition of employees to self-employment.

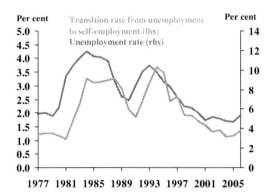

Correlation since 1977: +0.75

Source: ONS & Labour Force Survey microdata Spring quarters

Chart A.5 Rate of transition of unemployed to self-employment.

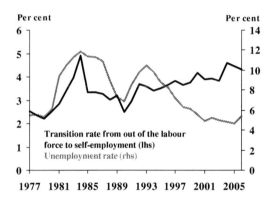

Correlation since 1977: +0.02

Source: ONS & Labour Force Survey microdata Spring quarters

Chart A.6 Rate of transition of OLF to self-employment.

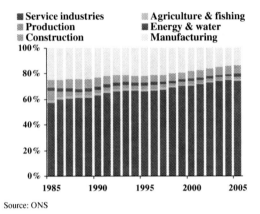

Source: ONS

Chart A.7 Contributions to total UK GVA.

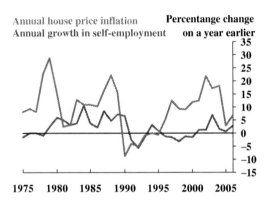

Source: Office for National Statistics & Nationwide house price data

Chart A.8 Nominal house price inflation and self-employment.

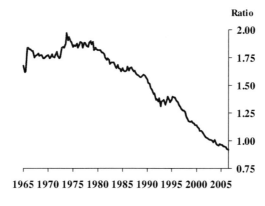

Source: ONS

Chart A.9 Ratio of business investment deflator to GDP deflator.

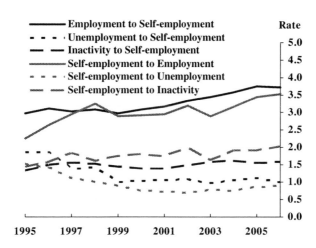

Source: LFS longitudinal dataset

Chart A.10 Transitions into and out of self-employment as a proportion of all self-employment.

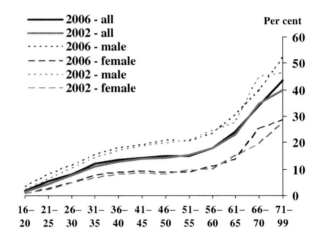

Source: Labour Force Survey Microdata

Chart A.11 Self-employment rates by age.

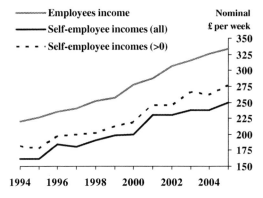

Source: Family Resources Survey

Chart A.12a Nominal incomes, medians.

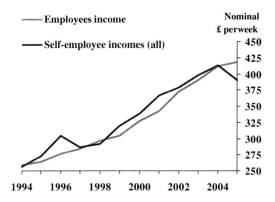

Source: Family Resources Survey

Chart A.12b Nominal incomes, means.

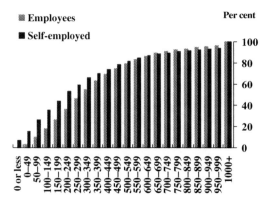

Source: Family Resources Survey

Chart A.13a Cumulative distribution of weekly incomes, 2003/2004, FRS.

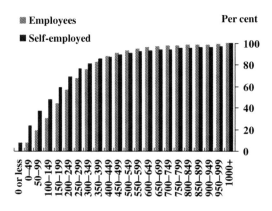

Source: Family Resources Survey

Chart A.13b Cumulative distribution of weekly incomes, 1994/1995, FRS.

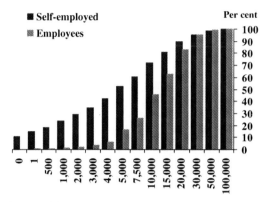

Source: HMRC

Chart A.14a Distribution of annual incomes, 2003/2004, SPI.

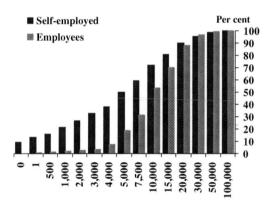

Source: HMRC

Chart A.14b Distribution of annual incomes, 1999/2000, SPI.

Source: Labour Force Survey microdata

Chart A.15 Age distributions, 2006.

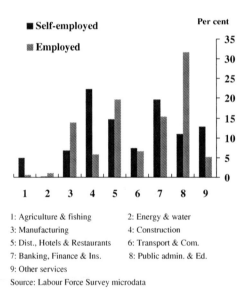

1: Agriculture & fishing   2: Energy & water
3: Manufacturing   4: Construction
5: Dist., Hotels & Restaurants   6: Transport & Com.
7: Banking, Finance & Ins.   8: Public admin. & Ed.
9: Other services

Source: Labour Force Survey microdata

Chart A.16 Self-employment by industry, 2006.

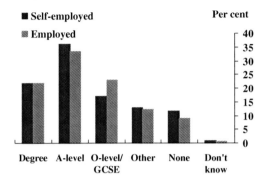

Source: Labour Force Survey microdata

Chart A.17 Education, 2006.

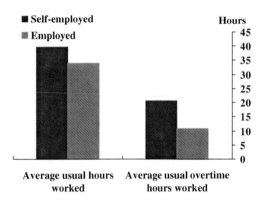

Source: Labour Force Survey microdata

Chart A.18 Weekly hours worked, 2006.

Acknowledgments

We thank Simon Parker and Jumana Saleheen for their helpful comments, and Philip Bunn and Nicola Dufty for their useful background research.

References

Acs, Z., D. Audretsch, and D. Evans (1994), 'The determinants of variations in self-employment rates across countries and over time'. Working Paper.

Bakhshi, H. and J. Thompson (2002), 'Explaining trends in UK business investment'. *Bank of England Quarterly Bulletin* (Spring), 33–41.

Bates, T. (1989), 'Small business viability in the urban ghetto'. *Journal of Regional Science* **29**(4), 625–643.

Benz, M. and B. S. Frey (2003), 'The value of autonomy; evidence from the self-employed in 23 countries'. Institute for Empirical Research in Economics, University of Zurich WP#173.

Bernhardt, I. (1994), 'Comparative advantage in self-employment and paid work'. *Canadian Journal of Economics* (May), 273–289.

Black, J., D. D. Meza, and D. Jeffreys (1996), 'House prices, the supply of collateral, and the enterprise economy'. *Economic Journal* **106**, 60–75.

Blanchflower, D. G. (2000), 'Self-employment in OECD countries'. *Labour Economics* **7**, 471–505.

Blanchflower, D. G. (2004), 'Self-employment: More may not be better'. *Swedish Economic Policy Review* **11**(2), 15–74.

Blanchflower, D. G. (2007a), 'The impact of the recent migration from Eastern Europe on the UK economy'. *Bank of England Quarterly Bulletin* **47**(1), 131–135.

Blanchflower, D. G. (2007b), 'Recent developments in the UK labour market'. *Bank of England Quarterly Bulletin* **47**(1), 158–172.

Blanchflower, D. G., P. Levine, and D. Zimmerman (2003), 'Discrimination in the small business credit market'. *Review of Economics and Statistics* **85**(4), 930–943.

Blanchflower, D. G. and A. J. Oswald (1998), 'What makes an entrepreneur?'. *Journal of Labor Economics* **16**(1), 26–60.

Blanchflower, D. G. and A. J. Oswald (2004), 'Wellbeing over time in Britain and the United States'. *Journal of Public Economics* **88**(7–8), 1359–1386.

Blanchflower, D. G., A. J. Oswald, and A. Stutzer (2001), 'Latent entrepreneurship across nations'. *European Economic Review* **45**(4–6), 680–691.

Blanchflower, D. G. and J. Wainwright (2005), 'An analysis of the impact of affirmative action programs on self-employment in the construction industry'. NBER Working Paper #11793.

Blau, D. (1987), 'A time-series analysis of self-employment in the United States'. *Journal of Political Economy* **95**, 445–467.

Borooah, V. K. and M. Hart (1999), 'Factors affecting self-employment among Indian and Black Caribbean men in Britain'. *Small Business Economics* **13**, 111–129.

Broussard, N., R. Chami, and G. Hess (2003), '(Why) do self-employed parents have more children?'. CESiFO Working Paper #1103.

Burke, A. E., F. R. Fitzroy, and M. A. Nolan (2000), 'When less is more: Distinguishing between entrepreneurial choice and performance'. *Oxford Bulletin of Economics and Statistics* **62**(5), 565–587.

Burke, A. E., F. R. Fitzroy, and M. A. Nolan (2002), 'Self-employment wealth and job creation: The roles of gender, non-pecuniary motivation and entrepreneurial ability'. *Small Business Economics* **19**, 255–270.

Campbell, M. and M. Daly (1992), 'Self-employment: Into the 1990s'. *Employment Gazette* (June), 269–291.

Cavalluzzo, K., L. Cavalluzzo, and J. Wolken (2002), 'Competition, small business financing and discrimination: Evidence from a new survey'. *Journal of Business* **75**, 641–679.

Clark, K. and S. Drinkwater (2000), 'Pushed out or pulled in? Self-employment among ethnic minorities in England and Wales'. *Labour Economics* **7**, 603–628.

Cowling, M. and P. Mitchell (1997), 'The evolution of UK self-employment: A study of government policy and the role of the macroeconomy'. *Manchester School of Economic and Social Studies* **65**(4), 427–442.

Di Tella, R., R. J. MacCulloch, and A. Oswald (2001), 'Preferences over inflation and unemployment: Evidence from surveys of happiness'. *American Economic Review* **91**, 335–341.

Dunn, T. A. and D. J. Holtz-Eakin (2000), 'Financial capital, human capital, and the transition to self-employment: Evidence from inter-generational links'. *Journal of Labor Economics* **18**(2), 282–305.

Ekelund, J., E. Johansson, M. R. Järvelin, and D. Lichterman (2005), 'Self-employment and risk aversion – evidence from psychological test data'. *Labour Economics* **12**(5), 649–659.

Evans, D. and B. Jovanovic (1989), 'An estimated model of entrepreneurial choice under liquidity constraints'. *Journal of Political Economy* **97**, 808–827.

Evans, D. and L. Leighton (1989), 'Some empirical aspects of entrepreneurship'. *American Economic Review* **79**, 519–535.

Fairlie, R. W. (1999), 'The absence of the African-American owned business: An analysis of the dynamics of self-employment'. *Journal of Labor Economics* **17**(1), 80–108.

Fairlie, R. W. (2002), 'Drug dealing and legitimate self-employment'. *Journal of Labor Economics* **20**(3), 538–567.

Fairlie, R. W. and H. A. Krashinsky (2006), 'Liquidity constraints, household wealth and entrepreneurship revisited'. Working Paper, University of California, Santa Cruz.

Fairlie, R. W. and B. D. Meyer (2000), 'Trends in self-employment among white and black men during the twentieth century'. *Journal of Human Resources* **XXXV**(4), 643–669.

Fairlie, R. W. and A. Robb (2005), 'Why are black-owned businesses less successful than white-owned businesses? He role of families, inheritances, and business human capital'. *Department of Economics.* UCSC. Paper 618.

Fairlie, R. W. and A. Robb (2006), 'Families, human capital, and small business: Evidence from the characteristics of business owners survey'. *Industrial and Labor Relations Review* **60**(2).

Freedman, J. (2001), 'Employed or self-employed?: Tax classification of workers in the changing labour market'. *The Institute for Fiscal Studies.* Discussion Paper.

Frey, B. S. and M. Benz (2002), 'Being independent is a great thing: Subjective evaluations of self-employment and hierarchy'. Institute for Empirical Research in Economics, University of Zurich WP#135.

Georgellis, Y., J. G. Sessions, and N. Tsitsianis (2005), 'Windfalls, wealth and the transition to self-employment'. *Small Business Economics* **25**(5), 407–428.

Green, F. and N. Tsitsianis (2005), 'An investigation of national trends in job satisfaction'. *British Journal of Industrial Relations* **43**(3), 401–429.

Hamilton, B. H. (2000), 'Does entrepreneurship pay? An empirical analysis of the returns to self-employment'. *Journal of Political Economy* **108**(3), 604–631.

Henley, A. (2005), 'Job creation by the self-employed: The roles of entrepreneurial and financial capital'. *Small Business Economics* **25**(2), 175–196.

Holtz-Eakin, D., D. Joulfaian, and H. S. Rosen (1994a), 'Entrepreneurial decisions and liquidity constraints'. *Journal of Political Economy* **102**, 53–75.

Holtz-Eakin, D., D. Joulfaian, and H. S. Rosen (1994b), 'Sticking it out: Entrepreneurial survival and liquidity constraints'. *Rand Journal of Economics* **25**(2), 334–347.

Holtz-Eakin, D. and H. S. Rosen (2005), 'Cash constraints and business startups: Deutschmarks versus dollars'. *BE Journals in Economic Analysis and Policy: Contributions to Economic Analysis and Policy* **4**(1), 1–26.

Hout, M. and H. S. Rosen (2000), 'Self-employment, family background and race'. *Journal of Human Resources* **15**(4), 670–692.

Hundley, G. (2001), 'Why and when are the self-employed more satisfied with their work?'. *Industrial Relations* **40**(2), 293–316.

Hurst, E. and A. Lusardi (2004), 'Liquidity constraints, household wealth, and entrepreneurship'. *Journal of Political Economy* **112**(2), 319–347.

Hyytinen, A. and O. Ruuskanen (2007), 'Time use of the self-employed'. *Kyklos* **60**(1), 105–122.

Johansson, E. (2000a), 'Self-employment and liquidity constraints: Evidence from Finland'. *Scandinavian Journal of Economics* **102**(1), 123–134.

Johansson, E. (2000b), 'Self-employment and the predicted earnings differential – Evidence from Finland'. *Finnish Economic Papers* **13**(1), 45–55.

Kidd, M. (1993), 'Immigrant wage differentials and the role of self-employment in Australia'. *Australian Economic Papers* **32**(60), 92–115.

Laferrere, A. and P. McEntee (1995), 'Self-employment and intergenerational transfers of physical and human capital: An empirical analysis of French data'. *Economic and Social Review* **27**(1), 43–54.

Lindh, T. and H. Ohlsson (1996), 'Self-employment and windfall gains: Evidence from the Swedish lottery'. *Economic Journal* **106**(439), 1515–1526.

Lindsay, C. and C. Macaulay (2004), 'Growth in self-employment in the UK'. *Labour Market Trends*. Office for National Statistics, October pp. 399–404.

Lyssiotou, P., P. Pashardes, and T. Stengos (2004), 'Estimates of the black economy based on consumer demand approaches'. *Economic Journal* **114**(497), 622–640.

Millard, S. (2000), 'The effects of increased labour market flexibility in the United Kingdom: Theory and practice'. *Bank of England*. Working Paper #109.

Parker, S. C. (2002), 'Do banks ration credit to new enterprises and should governments intervene?'. *Scottish Journal of Political Economy* **49**(2), 162–195.

Robson, M. T. (1998), 'Self-employment in the UK regions'. *Applied Economics* **30**, 313–322.

Taylor, M. (1996), 'Earnings, independence or unemployment? Why become self-employed?'. *Oxford Bulletin of Economics and Statistics* **58**(2), 253–266.

Taylor, M. (2001), 'Self-employment and windfall gains in Britain; evidence from panel data'. *Economica* **68**(272), 539–565.

Taylor, M. (2004), 'Self-employment in Britain: when, who and why?'. *Swedish Economic Policy Review* **11**(2), 141–173.

US Chamber of Commerce (2005), 'Access to capital; what funding sources work for you? Tables of survey results'. August, downloadable from http://www.uschamber.com/publications/reports/access_to_capital.htm.

Wainwright, J. (2000), *Racial discrimination and minority business enterprise: Evidence from the 1990 Census*, Studies in Entrepreneurship Series. New York and London: Garland Publishing.

Weir, G. (2003), 'Self-employment in the UK labour market'. *Labour Market Trends, ONS* **111**(9), 441–452.

Wolfers, J. (2003), 'Is business cycle volatility costly? Evidence from surveys of subjective well-being'. *International Finance* **6**(1), 1–26.

Yannis, G. and H. J. Wall (2005), 'Gender differences in self-employment'. *International Review of Applied Economics* **19**(3), 321–342.

Printed in the United Kingdom
by Lightning Source UK Ltd.
136277UK00002B/238/A

9 781601 980380